06221

D0489465

IMI *information service*
Sandyford, Dublin 16

THE TORTOISE

ALSO BY JOHN KAY

THE HARE & THE TORTOISE

An informal guide to business strategy

JOHN KAY

ep

THE ERASMUS PRESS

Copyright © John Kay

First published in Great Britain in 2006 by

The Erasmus Press Ltd
PO Box 4026
London W1A 6NZ

Individual articles from this book may be reproduced for
non-commercial purposes without specific permission
provided the source is acknowledged

The moral right of the author has been asserted

A catalogue record for this book is available
from the British Library

ISBN 0-9548093-1-9
ISBN 978-0-9548093-1-7

Designed by Briony Chappell
Illustrations by Graham Folwell
Printed in Great Britain by
Antony Rowe Ltd
Chippenham
Wiltshire

Contents

Preface

There are two ways to read this book. One is as a collection of essays written over the last decade, most of which appeared in columns in the *Financial Times*. Since all were written to stand alone, I hope the reader can dip into them with pleasure and even profit, and be reminded of one of the most extraordinary eras in business history. I have amended the original text to improve style and reduce duplication, but not to incorporate hindsight, though I have not been able to resist attaching commentary to some essays.

Alternatively, the book can be read from beginning to end, as a treatise on business strategy, based on what is now generally known as the resource-based theory. This approach defines the firm as a collection of capabilities and emphasises the match between these capabilities and the external environment within which the firm operates. This thesis on the nature of business success is developed steadily through the book; but along the way I take swipes at other perceptions, especially those that emphasise size, innovation and first mover advantages, and the role of charismatic leadership. The overall argument is summarised in the longest essay in the book, which appears second from last, and which can be read as introduction or conclusion.

But that chapter need not be read at all, by those who would treat the subject more lightly, and would rather just sample episodes in business life and laugh at the pretensions of business gurus and the claims of business executives whose self-importance exceeds their abilities. Not much that is written about business is enjoyable to read: neither the trivia that fills airport bookstalls nor the serious books which assert the scholarly credentials of the authors by their ponderous style. My objective has been to be more thoughtful than the former and more readable than the latter. This book has been fun to write and to compile. I hope the reader shares some of that enjoyment.

In search of strategy

If you are reading this book for pleasure, you will find in this section an attempt to draw lessons about business from a surprisingly wide range of sources – classical fables, the French philosopher Jacques Derrida, the failures of twentieth-century architecture, and the scientific dispute between incrementalists and saltationists.

If your goals are more earnest, and you are in search of instruction in business strategy, you will learn about the resource-based theory of strategy, acquire an evolutionary perspective on the development of the firm, and appreciate the relationship between them, recognise the strengths and limitations of the contribution of Michael Porter to current thinking about business, and gain a perspective on the purpose of corporate strategy and the nature of our knowledge of the business world.

The hare and the tortoise:
a fable for senior executives

5 SEPTEMBER 1997

Once upon a time, a tortoise lived in the marshes on the edge of a large plain. The tortoise had a hard shell with an attractive lustre and had lived there contentedly for many years.

But the tortoise was happy no longer. Its distress resulted from the athletics contests which were frequently organised by the animals of the plain. The tortoise did well in some events, like hide and seek and limbo dancing. But in every race, from the hundred metres to the cross country, the tortoise was left far behind by most of the other competitors. Especially by the hares.

What was to be done? Like everyone who is not sure what to do next, the tortoise turned to a firm of management consultants. It sought the advice of Boston, McBainey and Butterson, one of the best-regarded firms. Within a few days, the tortoise was surrounded by youngsters with MBAs from the finest business schools. They measured the dimensions of the tortoise and the way it moved. They held in-depth interviews with other tortoises, and with hares. Above all they listened intently to the tortoise's own concerns.

Following this intensive appraisal, Boston, McBainey and Butterson went away to prepare their recommendations. Soon the consultants returned to present their findings. This time they brought a senior partner and a van full of audio-visual equipment.

They began with their diagnosis. The reason the tortoise kept losing races, they pointed out, was that tortoises could not run as fast as hares. They illustrated this with several PowerPoint slides, and, conclusively, with a video that showed hares regularly overtaking tortoises. The tortoise was extremely impressed. 'I can see', it thought to itself, 'why these young people earn such high salaries. They have learnt to listen to the client and to focus exactly on the nature of its concerns.'

But there was better to come. The consultants went on to explain why the tortoise could not run as fast as the hare. It was because the tortoise had short legs and a heavy body. When you put diagrams of a tortoise and a hare side by side on the screen, there could be no doubt about it. The hare had much longer legs and a lean figure.

By this time, the tortoise was rolling on its shell in delight. These people did not, like some consultants, just relay back to you what you had already told them. The clincher was an elegant diagram that summarised it all. One axis described the length of legs; the other, body weight. The best position to be in was long legs, low body weight; the worst was short legs, high body weight. There was a picture of a hare, a tortoise, and an arrow to show how the tortoise needed to move, or re-engineer itself, as the consultants put it. 'What relevance! What insight!', the tortoise chortled.

Finally, the lights dimmed and the consultants moved to their recommendations. They showed the tortoise a picture of a jaguar. The elegance of the jaguar's graceful legs and slim body took the tortoise's breath away. So did their video which portrayed jaguars bounding across the plain, leaving hares trailing in the far distance. What the tortoise needed to do, the consultants explained, was to turn itself into a jaguar. Short legs were only superficial manifes-tations of the tortoise's problem. The real obstacle to success for the tortoise was that it was constrained by the limits of its imagination. So many creatures in today's environment, the consultants explained, suffered from this deficiency; so many had been helped, by Boston, McBainey and Butterson, to overcome it.

The consultants left their (rather large) invoice on the way out, but the tortoise's first reaction was that this had been money well spent. Yet after a few days, some doubts began to penetrate even

length of legs

body weight

Exhibit 1: Re-engineering for competitive success
The only diagram like this you will find in this book

the thick shell of the tortoise. Finally, it plucked up courage to telephone Boston, McBainey and Butterson. 'How exactly do I go about changing into a jaguar?', the tortoise asked.

Embarrassed at asking such a naïve question, the tortoise was relieved when the consultants offered an immediate answer. But then it remembered that good consultants always had an immediate answer. Many of our clients ask that, Boston, McBainey and Butterson explained; so many, in fact, that we have just set up a new change management division to help them. These consultants are trained to explain to every part of the body the importance of turning into a jaguar. Indeed, the new programme allows them to stay with a client for as long as necessary, until the change process is complete.

The tortoise was attracted by this proposition. But before returning the engagement letter to Boston, McBainey and Buttersons, it had a word with the wise old owl. And what the wise old owl told it was this. Tortoises and hares have evolved for very different environments. Hares do best in wide open spaces, where their speed gives them a competitive advantage. Tortoises survive for many years in hostile territory, where their shells protect them from predators and the weather. That is why even if the plains may sometimes look more attractive, they are attractive for hares, not for tortoises; and also why it is not sensible for hares to come down into the marshes. A happy creature is one whose characteristics match the environment within which it operates, and that is what the gradual process of biological evolution helps to achieve.

The tortoise thought this advice was shrewd, and trundled back into the marshes. It proved to be a wise decision. A few weeks later, a pride of lions found its way onto the plains, and ate all the hares. The tortoise lived on in the marshes, slowly but happily, almost ever after.

Made in Bavaria

17 FEBRUARY 1999

The history of BMW is as chequered as its blue and white badge. Blue and white are the colours of the state of Bavaria, where the company was founded over 80 years ago. For the first half of its life, BMW was mainly a manufacturer of aircraft engines. Its powerful motor bikes were also sought after, and it ventured into automobiles by manufacturing Austin Sevens under licence from their British designer.

In 1945 BMW was Germany's leading aero-engine manufacturer, as unfavourable a strategic position as any company has ever experienced. BMW's plight was still worse since its main production facility, at Eisenach, was located in the Soviet occupation zone.

The post-war recovery of German industry from the desolation of 1945 is still termed an economic miracle. There was no miracle for BMW, however. The company drifted, producing bubble cars (the BMW Gogomobile) that were not as much fun as those of its Italian rivals, and limousines that were not as stylish as those of its German competitors.

In 1959 BMW was on the edge of bankruptcy, and seemed certain to be absorbed by Mercedes. But after one of the longest and most extraordinary annual general meetings in the history of any company, Herbert Quandt emerged as BMW's dominant shareholder. The Quandt family still owns half the company's stock.

BMW was already planning its 1500 model when Quandt took control. Launched in 1962, this car established a new segment in the car market: the quality production saloon. The 1500 occupied a position between the ubiquitous mass production car and the craftsman-built output of the luxury producers. It filled a niche

Land of Herbert Quandt's cars

that BMW was almost uniquely placed to fill. The model drew on the company's ability to develop and use sophisticated technical skills in a production line workforce. This has been the source of competitive advantage for many German businesses and for the German economy as a whole.

Over the next two decades, BMW developed this market positioning and, in so doing, established the BMW brand with all the associations it retains today. BMW exemplifies two characteristics of powerful brands: quality certification and signalling. BMW cars have a reputation for build, for reliability and for low depreciation. And ownership of a BMW is a personal statement –

more stylish than a Volkswagen, more raffish than a Mercedes.

In common with a generation of German business men, Herbert Quandt did not seek to appear on the front cover of *Fortune* magazine. His public relations advisers were as much concerned to keep news out of the papers as to get it in. We will never know the balance of deliberation and luck in the determination of BMW's strategy. What we do know is that it is one of the great success stories in modern business history. And what we learn from it is the foundation of all successful corporate strategy – the match between the distinctive capabilities of the organisation and the market opportunities which it faces. That was what BMW, after many false starts in the twenty years after the war, finally achieved.

BMW's competitive advantage was bound to come under pressure as time went on. The quality of its production line engineering ceased to be such a distinctive capability. Not because that quality declined, but because other producers were better placed to emulate it. An element of BMW's success – and another common characteristic of successful strategy – was the development of a more enduring source of competitive advantage, the brand, in the window of opportunity created by a more transitory source of competitive advantage, engineering quality.

So what should BMW, faced with this growing pressure on its competitive advantages, have done? Strategy means understanding your distinctive capabilities and identifying markets where they can be turned into competitive advantages. The company was right to consider a move back into aero-engines, which reflected its – German – engineering capabilities and to a limited degree, exploited its brand. It was right to plan its American production facility in South Carolina, because that developed the brand in the American market. While it is still too early to judge the success of these ventures, they have strategic coherence. And perhaps BMW should use its domestic production capabilities, though not necessarily its brand, in other segments of the car market.

But instead of pursuing the logic of BMW's historic success – match market to competitive advantage – the company became a victim of the bland clichés of management jargon. It announced it was a supplier of mobility, rather than a manufacturer of cars, bikes and aero-engines. There is a profound misunderstanding here. The relevant links between these products are not that cars bikes and aero engines are all means of getting around but that they all use BMW's engineering skills and brand.

But more seriously, it fell for conventional but loose ideas on the importance of size and scale. 'BMW was too large to be a niche manufacturer, too small to be a volume producer' – as if failure to fit into the boxes of a consultant's slide presentation was evidence in itself of a strategic problem. 'BMW needed to achieve critical mass to be one of a handful of global players' – as if Rover itself had not demonstrated that size is no competitive advantage. And Pischetsrieder's plan for positioning Rover was to move it up market into a competitor for BMW itself. One way or another, this strategy was doomed to fail.

The question which a thoughtful student of Herbert Quandt's success would have asked is how BMW's competitive advantages – the quality of the workforce in its production facilities (in Germany), the power of its brand – were to be effectively deployed in the management of Rover. He would have concluded that they were not relevant if Rover was to continue to produce in the UK and trade under its own marque. And by pointing that out, would have saved the Quandt family many millions of euros.

British Leyland was formed in 1968 as the result of a government-sponsored merger of all remaining indigenous automobile producers. The company failed in 1974 and was taken into state ownership. Renamed Rover, it was bought in 1991 by BMW. In 1999, BMW sold Rover for a nominal sum to a private equity consortium. Rover finally closed in 2005. BMW continues to manufacture aero-engines (a joint venture with Rolls-Royce manufactures engines widely used in corporate jets) and to build cars in the United States.

Castles in the air

29 APRIL 1998

Architecture today is generally described as postmodern. It rejects the values which inspired the modern architecture of the 1950s and 1960s. You can still see these older values in buildings of that era: tall, grey, neglected and frequently awaiting demolition. Never before has the construction of an era been so short-lived.

Yet the architects who devised these buildings were not stupid or untalented people. The finest buildings of the founders of modern architecture – men like van der Rohe, Gropius, and le Corbusier – display genius to match the great architects of any era. But they were gripped by a theory of modernity – a theory encapsulated in le Corbusier's famous remark that 'a house is a machine for living in'. That philosophy reached its high point in the *unites d'habitation* in the outskirts of Marseilles – the world's first tower block, designed by le Corbusier.

The theory of modern architecture began by distancing itself from the past. For hundreds of years, architects had been constrained by principles of classical design, inherited from the Greeks and Romans. In this tradition houses are recognisably houses, whether Palladian villas or highland crofts, whether built by the Emperor Hadrian or George Wimpey. Any child asked to draw a house will immediately sketch an object with symmetrical windows arranged around a door beneath a sloping roof.

Modern architects, aided by modern technology, felt able to challenge all that. The only constraints were those of the imagination. It was time to rethink the purposes of a building from first principles on an entirely rational basis: literally from the ground up. So modern architects assumed a leadership role for themselves as harbingers of a new age. While Vanbrugh or Robert Adam had been tradesmen, sympathetic but marvellously skilful interpreters of the needs of their wealthy clients, the objective of the modernists was to drag us all kicking and screaming into the technological future.

And there was an emphasis on functionality. Buildings were to be stripped of anything that was not directly useful. Ornament was superficial, wasteful, and fundamentally dishonest. Buildings should be true to their essential purpose. And in these require-ments — modernity, rationalism and functionality — modern architects were resolutely supported by modern politicians and modern planners.

We now know that all this was a mistake. The leading theorist of postmodern architecture, Charles Jencks, dates the end of the modern era from 1972, when the city of St Louis demolished the Pruitt-Igoe apartment blocks which had received architectural prizes only seventeen years before. Since then, municipalities and firms all over the world have followed this example.

The point, of course, is that houses are not just machines for living in. They are homes and parts of communities. To serve these needs demands respect for conventional — even banal — aesthetics and for the structures of social relationships that make homes and communities. The tower blocks, with their emphasis on function-ality, earned little respect from their inhabitants who urinated in the lifts, painted graffiti on the walls, and quickly destroyed even the prized functionality.

Now no-one would make these mistakes today. Or would they? If you want a clue as to who might, take a look at the buildings erected by modern corporations: rational, modern, functional and almost uniformly undistinguished. The greatest of new corporate headquarters are probably those of AT&T and HSBC. Exceptions which prove the rule: these structures were built by firms which were able to stand back a little from the pressures of competitive markets. Perhaps the only recent UK corporate headquarters of any architectural interest is the Lloyds building, and thereby hangs a tale. No British company today has the self-confidence exuded by the massive piles which ICI and Unilever erected between the wars on the banks of the Thames.

Gropius and le Corbusier would feel strangely at home in today's boardrooms. Have you ever heard a chief executive emphasise the need for a company to distance itself from the past, and rethink the nature of its activities from first principles? Have you ever heard a chief executive say it is no longer enough to lead from behind, that it is no longer enough for leaders of modern management to understand the evolution of their organisation and exemplify that evolution: that today it is necessary to define a vision and lead everyone in the company towards it?

And have you ever heard a chief executive say that the modern company must be lean and mean, and that any part of it that cannot be justified in strict functional terms must be eliminated? Come to think of it, have you ever heard a recent speech from a chief executive that has not said all of these things?

Now maybe there is a difference between the architecture of buildings and the architecture of organisations. Maybe it is true that the functionality of buildings depends, in the long run, on intangible aspects of the relationship

...and of Ludwig's castles

between the buildings and the occupants, things which cannot be easily articulated but had been learnt from generations of experience: but that the same is not true of the functionality of corporations. Maybe it is true that while we may destroy communities when we restructure them without regard to the wishes of their members, the same is not true when we restructure corporations. Or maybe there are no such differences, and the architects of modern companies are repeating the errors of the architects of modern buildings.

Business heroes

JACQUES DERRIDA

9 NOVEMBER 2004

'Il n'y a pas de hors texte'

Jacques Derrida (1930–2004), Algerian-born French philosopher
and literary critic. Professor of philosophy at the École Normale
Supérieure, Director of Studies at the École des Hautes Études en
Sciences Sociales at Paris, and Professor of Humanities at the
University of California (Irvine).

'No one in the lunch room has ever heard of him. I can look him up on Google if you like'. When *The Guardian* newspaper sought tributes to Jacques Derrida, who died last month, that was the best the City of London could do. President Chirac of France described him as 'one of the major figures in the intellectual life of our time', itself enough to create apoplexy at the *Wall Street Journal*. Derrida's thought, the *Journal* said, 'deserves unstinting criticism from anyone who cares about the moral fabric of intellectual life'.

Derrida was a leading figure in postmodernism, and his most famous idea was deconstruction, his mantra 'there is nothing but the text'. As child actor, I once played the messenger in *Waiting for Godot*. Samuel Beckett's masterpiece is not easy for anyone to understand, and not at all easy if you are ten years old. I formed a plan to write to Beckett, explain my predicament, and ask him to tell me what the play was about. But Google had not been invented then, and I never managed to find the playwright's address.

I now know Beckett was in Paris, perhaps consorting with Derrida in some left bank café. Jacques would have told the author how to reply. Reread the play of course: 'There is nothing but the text'. A play is not a textbook. The purpose of reading a video recorder manual is to deduce the intentions of the writer, and we judge the manual by how easy it is to interpret those intentions. If you lost the manual, you could, with sufficient skill and effort, reproduce its content. A video recorder is a material device with specific and unchanging functions.

But there is no similarly simple relationship between intention and function in a play. If Shakespeare had wanted to warn of the perils of ambition, he could have used auto content wizard to prepare a PowerPoint presentation rather than engage in writing Richard III. The play he did write has many levels of meaning and can sustain many interpretations. What you learn from it is personal. The child prodigy Jedediah Buxton, asked what he thought of *Richard III*, observed (correctly) that the play contained

12,445 words. He had seen the same play as everyone else, yet a different one. Shakespeare no doubt thought of *Richard III* in terms of his royalties. All these perspectives are valid, none complete, and none, not even Shakespeare's, uniquely privileged.

But we think of businesses as if they were static machines like video recorders rather than evolving, complex entities like plays. I have often described some episode in business history, only to be told by a member of the audience 'I was there, and this is how it really was'. But insiders have no special insight into how it really was: only one, necessarily limited and prejudiced, perspective. Business journalists believe they learn the truth about a company by interrogating its chief executive, making the same childish mistake as I did in seeking advice from Samuel Beckett. And with less justification: Beckett wrote every word of *Waiting for Godot*, but no CEO can ever aspire to that degree of control over his organisation.

The cynical claim from old Europe that there is no ultimate truth about human affairs explains the ire of the *Wall Street Journal*, whose editorial pages proclaim that truth every day. But there is no one true story, only more and less useful interpretation. The financial statements of Enron and Parmalat may have been, in some literal sense, true, but these accounts were intended to mislead. We understand such companies better still by gaining understanding of the psychology of greed and the anthropology of small Italian towns.

A business history, like a profound play, has many strands, and when one is identified many more remain to be disentangled. When Harvard MBA students discuss case studies, they are told there is no right answer to the questions they will debate. I doubt they realise they are engaged in deconstruction. But, class, I like to think that Derrida would have approved.

Honda's rising sun

16 NOVEMBER 2004

Honda and the Supercub is probably the best known and most debated case in business strategy. In the 1950s, motor-cycles were sold through specialist outlets welcoming only testosterone-loaded young men. Bikes were powerful and noisy and the leather clothes of their riders smelt of leaking oil. Honda entered the US market in 1959 and changed everything. Five years later that company made one in two bikes sold in the US. Their best-selling machine was the 50cc Supercub, sold by sports retailers. The company's advertising slogan was 'you meet the nicest people on a Honda'.

The story benefits from deconstruction. One school of explanation derives from the original Harvard Business School case study. That case is itself based on a 1975 report by the Boston Consulting Group for the British government. The report described these events as the archetype of orchestrated attack on Western markets by Japanese manufacturers of consumer goods. Having established large economies of scale in the domestic market, Honda was able to exploit its unassailable cost advantage globally.

A different history was given by Richard Pascale, who travelled to Tokyo to interview the by then elderly Japanese who had managed Honda's first steps in the United States. These executives explained that Honda had never imagined that small bikes would find a market in the open spaces of the United States. The company had focused on large machines, planning to compete with established US manufacturers. Mr Honda, they said, was especially confident of success with these products because the shape of the handlebars looked like the eyebrows of Buddha.

But the eyebrows of Buddha were not appealing in the world of Marlon Brando and James Dean. The Japanese hawked their wares around the Western United States, to dealers 'who treated us discourteously and, in addition, gave the general impression of being motor-cycle enthusiasts who, secondarily, were in business'. The few machines they sold, ridden more aggressively than was possible in Japan, leaked even more oil than their US counterparts.

Dispirited and short of foreign currency, the Japanese imported some Supercubs to ease their own progress around the asphalt jungle of Los Angeles. Passers-by expressed interest, and eventually a Sears buyer approached them. And the 'nicest people' slogan? That was invented by a University of California undergraduate on summer assignment.

Only the naïve will believe either account. Successful business strategy is a mixture of luck and judgment, opportunism and design, and even with hindsight the relative contributions of each cannot be disentangled. Mr Honda was an irascible genius who made inspired intuitive decisions – with considerable assistance from the meticulous market analysis of his colleagues and the intense discipline of Honda's production line operations.

It is a mistake to believe that the ultimate truth about Honda could ever be established through diligent research and rigorous debate. The BCG/Harvard account, though paranoid, is right to emphasise Honda's operational capabilities. Pascale correctly stresses the human factors, but how his interviewees must have laughed as they watched him write down the story of the eyebrows of Buddha. Andrew Mair's survey illustrates how, as Jacques Derrida would have anticipated, every academic and consultant – including me – interpreted the Honda story in the light of his own preconceptions.

The Boston Consulting Group naturally saw the experience curve at work and later, when peddling a different panacea, identified an example of time-based competition. Gary Hamel and C.K. Prahalad perceived the development of Honda's 'core competence' in engine manufacture. Henry Mintzberg seized on Pascale's account as an instance of emergent strategy.

For me the lesson of Honda is that a business with a distinctive capability which develops innovative products that exploit that capability and recognises the appropriate distribution channels for that innovation, can take the world by storm. And that lesson is valid whether Honda's achievement was the result of planning or serendipity. There no true story and no point in debating what the true story might be.

Business heroes

MICHAEL PORTER

The Five Forces

Michael Porter (1947–) has been at Harvard since 1969, where he joined the faculty after completing an MBA in the Business School and a Ph.D. in the economics department. In 1980, he published his most famous work, *Competitive Strategy*, which describes 'the five forces', followed by *Competitive Advantage* (1985) and *The Competitive Advantage of Nations* (1992).

On the north bank of the Charles River lies the academic city of Cambridge, Massachusetts. To the south lies the busy metropolis of Boston. Around twenty years ago, a young man crossed one of the many bridges which span the Charles River. He carried in his briefcase the plans of his former employer. He hoped that these would form the basis of his future career in the rich but demanding environment to the south. Discarding all evidence of his previous identity, he found succour in an office in Soldier's Field. His gamble paid off. Within a few years, he had found fame and fortune beyond the dreams of his former colleagues.

The young man was Michael Porter. The institution he left was the economics department of Harvard University. The institution in which he took refuge was the Harvard Business School. The plans he brought with him described what had become known as the structure-conduct-performance paradigm (SCP). The fame and fortune which followed are well known.

The structure of SCP is shown in Figure 1, drawn from what still remains its bible, the magisterial survey by F. M. Scherer. Figure 1

FIGURE 1: *A Model of Industrial Analysis*

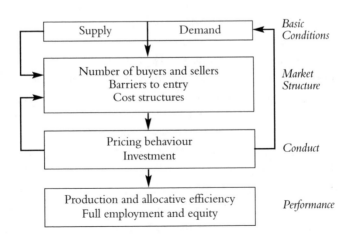

Source: Simplified from Scherer and Ross (1990)

begins from basic conditions of supply and demand in an industry. The SCP paradigm asserts that these conditions determine the structure of the market and industry, and this competitive structure influences the behaviour of firms and dictates the performance of the industry. It provides a coherent framework which permits a logical ordering of the many influences on industries and markets.

SCP explains how structure influences conduct and performance. The criteria of performance are those of public policy: full employment, efficiency and equity. A business analyst looks at norms of business success – profits, revenues, market shares. But these are not what interested Scherer. His Harvard colleagues were much in demand as advisers to government, particularly the anti-trust division of the Department of Justice, but were only rarely consulted by senior executives.

If they *had* been consulted by senior executives, there would have been severe constraints on what they were able to say. The SCP approach fails to explain, or even to address, the central question of business strategy. Why do some firms do better than others, operating in the same environment? If two firms each face the same basic conditions of supply and demand, if both firms operate within the same market structure, why should there be any difference in their performance?

Porter's achievement – in his first book, *Competitive Strategy*, was to communicate with an audience directed to profit rather than public service. He rewrote the SCP framework in terms which were directed at, and accessible to, business people. The affinity between the SCP framework of Figure 1, and Porter's famous five forces (Figure 2), is immediately obvious. Industrial economics had become business strategy.

But Porter's translation did not resolve, and could not resolve, the second weakness of the SCP approach. Why did some firms manage the five forces better than others? Porter's framework is consequently more successful in his first book – *Competitive*

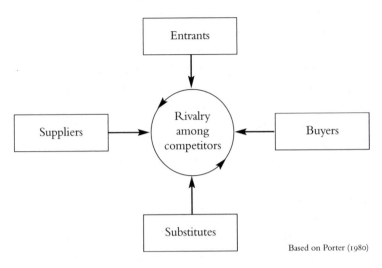

FIGURE 2: *The Five Forces*

Entrants

Suppliers

Rivalry
among
competitors

Buyers

Substitutes

Based on Porter (1980)

Strategy – which is mostly concerned with the structure and behaviour of industries and markets, than in his second – *Competitive Advantage* – which attempts to focus more closely on issues which affect individual firms.

It is ironic, but hardly surprising, that in his third work – *The Competitive Advantage of Nations* – Porter reverted to the traditional concerns of Harvard economists. That book is mostly directed to public policy. And to do so he trawled back to the concepts of an even earlier generation of economists. It was Marshall and Pigou, (from Cambridge, England) who had first described the growth of industries and markets by describing clusters of firms and who had emphasised the importance of external economies – cost advantages which arise when many firms succeed in the same industry.

But while Michael Porter was teaching strategy on the Boston side of the Charles River, something new was happening on the other bank. They do not teach the SCP paradigm in the Harvard economics programme any more. SCP has given way to a new style of industrial economics that emphasises topics such as asymmetric information – how markets work, and often don't work, when sellers know more about what they sell than buyers about what they buy. It uses game theory to understand how small groups of competitors interact. It deals with contracts, relationships, and describes how incentive structures influence the behaviour of principals and agents.

And in Cambridge, England, an economist called Edith Penrose had laid the basis of the resource-based theory of strategy. In which firms are not – as in SCP and the five forces – black boxes whose internal workings are unexplained, but are dynamic collections of capabilities. It recognised the most important economic fact of the last century – the existence of large firms.

But mostly, the new economists wrote in mathematics, preferring the esteem of their peers to the rewards of the business guru. Still, the rewards of the guru are not to be sniffed at. Perhaps a few more people should cross the river?

Distinctive capabilities

25 OCTOBER 1996

One of the most used and abused phrases in business strategy is 'core competencies'. Nowadays, it has simply become a pretentious phrase for activities – things a business does do, or would like to do.

The disease has even struck my own company. Last week I picked up a sheet that proudly proclaimed that the competencies of London Economics include economic knowledge, business experience, analytical skills, problem solving, industry knowledge, innovation, project management and customer focus. That list is a terrible muddle. It conflates the organisation's resources – its economic knowledge and business experience – with things the organisation does – problem solving and project management – and with characteristics we need in our business, but probably don't have – innovation and customer focus.

But it is a list not very different from the list generated by most companies. One firm I know claimed to have no less than forty-three core competencies. It's time to think more clearly – in your firm as well as mine.

The phase 'core competencies' is derived from an influential *Harvard Business Review* article by C. K. Prahalad and Gary Hamel, which is a popularisation of what has become known over the last decade as the resource-based theory of strategy. The term resource-based theory, in turn, seems to originate in a 1984 article in the *Strategic Management Journal* by Bo Wernerfelt; and the ideas it describes were in turn first effectively expounded twenty years earlier in a jewel of a volume called *The Theory of the Growth of the Firm* by Edith Penrose. I mention this history partly to emphasise that the best ideas in management are rarely the newest and also to stress that what really matters is not the words we use but the thinking that lies behind them. We can debate for ever whether something is or is not a core competence but unless we know why the answer matters the debate is a waste of everyone's time.

There is a key distinction between what the firm is − the resources it has, like economic knowledge and business experience − and the things it does − like problem solving and project management. The essential strategic question for any firm is how well its capabilities match its activities, and if you muddle the two you can't even begin to answer that question effectively. The resource-based-theory of strategy emphasises that each firm is characterised by its own individual collection of resources.

And in looking at these resources, it is necessary to draw a line between those resources which are truly idiosyncratic to that firm and those which can be readily bought in the market place. The Coca-Cola brand is unique to the company, but fizzy drink technology is available to anyone. I have called this the difference between distinctive capabilities and skills, but the terms are not important: what is important is the different ideas they express.

Any but the most transitory of competitive advantages has to be based on distinctive capabilities. A competitive advantage based only on skills − those resources of the firm which others can go out and buy − will quickly be eliminated. If such skills yield profits, others will go out and buy the same resources. So Coca-Cola's competitive advantage is based on its Coke brand, not its fizzy drink technology.

You can buy the skills incorporated in Marks & Spencer (others have, by poaching their employees), but competitors cannot attack the company's competitive advantage because they cannot buy its distinctive capabilities − its structure of relationships and its reputation with customers. And correspondingly, when Marks & Spencer wants to apply a distinctive capability − its reputation with customers − in a new market such as financial services, it can go out and buy the financial services skills it needs. There is no shortage of people who know how to design a personal equity plan or process a life insurance policy.

So what is needed in defining a firm's strategy is to identify the markets and activities in which the firm's distinctive capability is relevant, and then put together the skills needed to capture these markets and perform these activities. No firm will ever have forty-three distinctive capabilities. It is rare for any company to have more than one or two. Sometimes a firm may have none at all. In that case, it will not have any competitive advantages and will do well to make an average return on capital. That hard but obvious truth is often difficult to accept.

London Economics' distinctive capabilities lie in the company's technical skills in economics, and an established position, especially in the recruitment market, which makes it difficult for others to replicate that stance. That means we should only try to sell work which could only be done by someone with exceptional abilities in economics. Other reasons offered for pursuing new lines of business − that market is growing, this market is very profitable, we could do it − should all be rejected. Even if we could do these things, if they don't match our distinctive capability we won't make money in them for long. And because it's hard to reproduce our distinctive capability, I don't mind telling readers of the *Financial Times* what it is.

And so there will never be any successful generic strategies for companies. The real competencies of firms are their distinctive capabilities and these are few in number and individual in nature. Any effective strategy is specific to the firm that deploys it.

London Economics is the consultancy business which I founded in 1986 and of which I was executive chairman until 1996. And while rivals could not emulate Marks & Spencer's distinctive capabilities, Marks & Spencer could erode them − and was in process of doing so − see page 76.

Natura non facit saltum

9 JUNE 1999

I once wrote a fable about a tortoise which, upset by its slow though persistent performance, tried to turn itself into a jaguar. My purpose was to poke fun at the management consultants and visionary CEOs who peddle exaggerated nostrums for transformational change in organisations. I didn't know that evolutionary biologists had considered carefully whether such transformational change could occur. At high table in Oxford, I have since learnt of the dispute between the saltationists and the incrementalists.

Incrementalists believe that the evolution of species occurs as the result of a series of small, almost imperceptible, steps. The saltationists take their name from *saltum*, the Latin word for jump. Their thesis is that species continue unchanged for many generations. Occasionally, a chance mutation might lead to a major improvement which would then spread rapidly through the population.

The battle between incrementalists and saltationists is now over, and few serious scientists are to be found in the saltationist camp today. But the analogy between the development of business organisation and the evolution of species is sufficiently close for it to be instructive to understand why the saltationists thought as they did, and why they were wrong. And since there are still many saltationists in the business world, the discrediting of their scientific counterparts should give us all pause for thought.

The evidence that supported the saltationist position was the appearance of large gaps in the fossil record. We did not seem to see enough intermediate cases to support incrementalism. But was this phenomenon real, or simply a feature of the limitations of the evidence and the discernment of those who examined that evidence? Time has suggested that the discontinuities are in the evidence rather than in the world.

And other knowledge has clarified the deficiencies of saltationism. Large mutations in species, even if useful, die out. We might wish we had eyes in the back of our head, and they would indeed be of value. They would greatly reduce the probability of being mugged and it would be easier to find a taxi when hurrying along the pavement on a wet day.

But in reality a child with eyes in the back of its head would be a horrible freak. Many other physical adaptations would be necessary for such a creature to function, and many of these adaptations would not be made well. The child would have other physical disadvantages, and recurrent medical problems. Not meeting the conventional standards of attractiveness, it would be unlikely to find a mate. Would you marry someone with eyes in the back of their head?

But the outlook is brighter, as well as more extensive, for someone with a slightly wider field of vision than average. Such people are less likely to die in traffic accidents. They have a better chance of seeing their ideal partner on the opposite side of the room at a party. So evolution does favour genes for slighter wider fields of vision. Over time, this means that our descendants will probably see better than we do.

Incremental innovations often succeed but discontinuous ones only rarely. The great biologist R. A. Fisher used the following example. Imagine a microscope whose focus is not quite right. If you make a small adjustment, then there is a fifty per cent chance that this is an improvement. But for a big change, there is almost no chance that the result will be better. Might the same be true for organisations?

The analogy is illuminating because there is a key assumption in Fisher's illustration. It depends on the focus being almost right to begin with. If the focus is hopeless, any change is as unlikely to be successful as any other. Fisher's assumption necessarily holds for species – a species that is not approximately suited to its environment will be extinct.

And Fisher's assumption holds for companies as well. A firm that is not approximately suited to its environment will be out of business. Which makes these CEOs who wish to redesign their companies in line with some abstract organisational blueprint, or some theory of what tomorrow's markets will be like, the business analogue of impatient children who grab the focus wheel on the microscope.

Now there are some companies which find themselves at odds with their environment – which are not even nearly in focus. Mostly, this is because they have faced some discontinuity. Privatised companies, brought up in a world in which they needed to adapt to the dictates of politicians rather than the needs of customers, may suddenly be required to cope with a competitive environment. Or firms whose market has seen fundamental change, as when the computer market shifted from mainframes to PCs and left IBM's competitive advantages stranded.

Most of the examples of successful organisational transformation which form the basis of business school case studies – like IBM or British Airways – emerged from circumstances like these. The evolutionary analogy tells us that this happens only rarely. We use the dinosaur to exemplify extinction rather than adaptation. But it too provides an instructive analogy.

We are still not sure why dinosaurs died, though the favoured hypothesis today is that an asteroid hit the earth and changed the climate. And if that is right, there was nothing the dinosaurs could have done, even if they had anticipated the asteroid's arrival. Evolution continued, of course, but we are descended from apes, not dinosaurs. The development of industrial structures is similar. Such structures change over time, but less through the adaptation of old firms than by the evolution of new ones. So the computer industry today is dominated, not by a transformed IBM, but by the more recently established Microsoft.

Talking about strategy

5 AUGUST 1998

No self-respecting business today would be without a strategy. But the modern student of business is often confused by the many different uses of the words strategy and strategic.

Probably the commonest sense in which the word strategy is employed today is as a synonym for expensive. You can always be sure this meaning is intended when the context involves advice. Here are some examples. 'We are strategy consultants', 'Can we help you with your strategy?' 'I advise company x on its strategy'. These can be interpreted respectively as 'our fees are very high', 'we hope to send you a large bill' and 'company x pays me a lot of money'. Another useful term is 'strategy weekend' which means 'a lot of people eating good food and drinking fine wine at a country house hotel'.

Strategy means expensive is also the key to understanding phrases like 'strategic investment' and 'strategic acquisition'. 'This is a strategic investment' should be translated as 'we are going to lose a lot of money on this project'. 'This is a strategic acquisition' means 'we are paying more for this company than it is worth.'

The word strategy is also often used to mean important. You can recognise this in the phrase 'I'm in strategy' which means 'I have a large office, large salary, and the ear of the chief executive'. 'An interesting proposal, but does it have strategic significance?' can be translated as 'I am not going to waste my time on this'. And when accountants, the human resources department, and public relations people explain how they need to be involved in the firm's strategic planning, what they are saying is that they don't receive enough attention.

The Strategy Weekend, after Hogarth

Strategy is 'what the chief executive does'. Thus 'Mr A deals with the strategic issues while Ms B is concerned with operations' means 'Mr A has a much larger salary and many more share options than Ms B'. Importance is, of course, a relative concept, specific to the environment of the firm. What is important is what the important people do. Since their focus is often on strategy rather than operations, running the business is not necessarily important.

Sometime strategy is about acquisitions and disposals. This interpretation is universal in the City. 'We don't understand company x's strategy' means 'we haven't heard about (or aren't hired for) any deals involving company x'. 'Firm y has no strategy' means 'Firm y hasn't bought or sold other companies recently'. This concept is reflected in the common financial market term 'corporate activity', which covers financial restructuring and acquisitions. The opposite of 'corporate activity' is 'corporate inactivity', which describes a company's operations – making things and encouraging customers to buy them.

So what is strategy, really? The strategic issues facing a company fall into two groups. Corporate strategy is about answering the question 'what markets are we (or should we) be in?' Business strategy, or competitive strategy, is about how the company is placed in these markets relative to its competitors.

So the subject of corporate strategy is the matching of the capabilities of the firm to the external environment that it faces. The first stage in considering strategy is to determine what these capabilities are. Firms can add value only if they can do something in a market that others cannot easily replicate. Thus the successful corporation is generally built round – no more than one or two – things that it is uniquely able to do. Sometimes these distinctive capabilities are based on innovation, sometimes on reputation – with customers, suppliers or in the labour market. Sometimes they are based on the structure of a firm's relationships, its architecture, either within the firm and outside it. When you have analysed your distinctive capabilities, you can identify those markets in which they add value – and those in which they do not.

And this analysis tends to frame your analysis of business unit strategy as well. Should you be positioned up or down market of your principal competitors? This is another question whose answer depends on your distinctive capabilities. How should you respond to their initiatives – in pricing, in marketing, in product innovation? Answers to these questions are based partly on what differentiates you from them – distinctive capabilities again – and partly on an appreciation of the interactions between small groups of competitors.

And because strategy is based on distinctive capabilities, there are no generic strategies. There really are many interpretations of strategy. Strategy is what is right for you.

Does size matter?

No idea about business is more persistent than the notion that scale is critical to efficiency and effectiveness. The essays in this section argue that size is the product, not the cause, of business success and consider the military analogy which is so much in the minds of those who believe that fortune favours the biggest battalions.

Global players only

27 MARCH 2003

I've heard it from people who make pharmaceuticals and from people who make defence equipment. From executives in utilities and executives in advertising. Among banks and law firms. From telecommunications companies and media businesses. They all expect their industry to develop in the same way as automobiles. In an increasingly globalised marketplace, maturing industries will become steadily more concentrated. Only a small number of big players will survive.

There is one problem with these analogies. What is said about the motor industry is not true. The peak of concentration in automobile production was reached in the early 1950s, and since then there has been a substantial decline. In the late 1960s, when globalisation of the industry began in earnest, the big three car manufacturers – General Motors, Ford and Chrysler – made half the world's cars. Today's big three – GM, Ford and Toyota – together have 36% of world output.

However you look at it, small car makers have been steadily gaining market share at the expense of large ones. Back in the 1960s, the ten largest car makers had a market share of 85%; today it is around 75%. Nine companies made more than a million vehicles in 1969: fourteen did so last year. Fifteen companies produced more than 1% of world output in 1969. Seventeen companies have more than 1% of world output today.

Concentration has fallen even though weak firms have repeat-edly been absorbed through mergers. Daimler has taken over Chrysler, Renault has allied with Nissan, and Ford has acquired Volvo. These transactions have stayed the decline in the share of large car makers, for the first time in a generation. But since few of these combinations are doing well, the downward trend is likely to resume.

People in business continue to deliver clichés about critical mass and global players although, with another part of their brains, they don't really believe it. When they talk about General Motors they usually also employ words like inflexible, bureaucratic, or even dinosaur, and they buy Hondas because they think Honda makes better cars. Honda entered the automobile industry in 1967, the same year that the British government insisted domestic firms merge to form British Leyland – a business with the critical mass to be a global player.

The evolution of the world car industry has followed a complex pattern, although one that is common to many other products. The hundreds, perhaps thousands, of small car manufacturers at the beginning of the twentieth century mostly went out of business or were absorbed into larger firms. They simply weren't good enough to compete with the few companies that managed to master the technology and understand the market. Cars were still formidably expensive, and low costs were vital. But cheapness ceased to be the most important competitive advantage in the auto industry as early as the 1920s. Henry Ford, who would give you any colour you wanted so long as it was black, was overtaken by GM, which would give you any colour you wanted.

As markets evolve, differentiation becomes steadily more important. Better margins are made from specialist vehicles which cater for the differentiated tastes of rich customers. Sports utility vehicles, aimed at people who dream of a rugged outdoor lifestyle very different from the one they actually lead, have been the lifeblood of the car business in the past decade.

Globalisation allows small producers which develop competitive advantages to deploy them on a world scale. That is how Toyota was able to grow from an unimportant Japanese maker of textile machinery into one of the big three world auto manufacturers. Mercedes and BMW, rather than outgrowing their market niches, were able to develop them on a world scale.

The growth of companies such as these has led to a decline in concentration in the automobile industry. Yet all of them are likely to be overtaken in turn by new specialist producers whose names have not yet come to our attention. Success in the motor industry comes, not from size and scale, but from developing competitive advantages in operations and marketing these competitive advantages internationally. The same is true in pharmaceuticals and defence equipment, utilities and advertising, banking and legal services, telecommunications and media.

The car that ran out of road

22 MARCH 2005

Chief executives across industry have followed Jack Welch's famous maxim: unless you are number one or two in your industry, you are dead. There used to be a phrase for it – 'to be the General Motors of this industry'. Not any more. Last week, GM forecast yet another set of disappointing results. The rating agencies threaten to call its securities junk. The company's market share today is lower than when founder Billy Durant was slogging it out with Henry Ford. But it is not Ford, GM's long-term rival, which has benefited from this fall but Toyota, Hyundai, and prospectively Shanghai Motors.

Still, General Motors survives as an independent company. No one much wants its assets, and even less its liabilities: the United Auto Workers' trades union and the pension and medical benefits of retired employees. Another American icon will soon disappear altogether. American Telephone and Telegraph (AT&T), will be swallowed by one of its offspring, SBC.

For most of the twentieth century, AT&T and GM were the most powerful corporations in the United States. They acquired these positions by overtaking the product of the greatest consolidation of all: US Steel, once the largest company in the world. It is many years since that company ceased to be a significant force, even in the steel industry.

The failures at GM and AT&T didn't happen because these companies were big. General Motors ran into difficulties because it no longer made the cars its customers wanted, because the company was slow to see how preferences were changing, and because production systems could not match the cost levels and reliability achieved by Asian and European competitors.

AT&T used market dominance to achieve technical excellence. Then deregulation removed its monopolies and the settlement of an anti-trust suit removed its local franchises. The corporation was freed to pursue opportunities in the convergence of telecommunications and computing, but inspired vision was marred by inept execution. The company was repeatedly outsmarted by upstart rivals in its core telecommunications markets.

No, GM and AT&T didn't fail because they were big. They failed because they were insufficiently sensitive to new consumer requirements, because they responded too slowly to changing market structures, because their organisations were too bureaucratic to see what their nimbler competitors were doing. But all these things were direct consequences of their scale of operations.

We overestimate the power of scale in business because the advantages of size are technological and tangible, the disadvantages human and intangible. The disadvantages seem avoidable – large firms needn't become inflexible, divorced from their customers, overloaded by long bureaucratic chains of command. Or so books such as *When Giants Learn to Dance* would tell us. But giants don't often learn to dance, and when they do the effort quickly exhausts them. The few long-lived giants are either firms that have changed a lot, or in industries that have changed little.

General Electric has learned not to dance, but to shift venue whenever the band is playing the wrong tune. Its main businesses today, in financial services, aircraft engines and medical equipment, are quite different from those that gave the company its name. Exxon and Shell once tapped oil shale and sold petrol in cans at the roadside. Today they drill beneath the ocean. But competition and market structure has been more stable in oil than in any other major industry.

These businesses are the exceptions in a world of which GM and AT&T are more typical. Aspire to be number one or two. But harbour no illusions that such positions are likely to be sustained.

The plane that fell to earth

10 DECEMBER 2003

I used to teach students that no dominant position was so entrenched as Boeing's grip on the civil aviation market. Incumbent firms can see off even potentially stronger competitors through three strategic advantages. Economies of scale – lower costs from larger output. Sunk costs – historic expenditures that yield future benefits. Economies of scope – cost or revenue advantages from operating in related markets.

Boeing had all three. Scale economies in plenty – Boeing's Seattle facility, and the Airbus assembly plant at Toulouse, are reputed to be the largest single structures in their respective continents. A powerful experience curve – the cost of producing any particular line of aircraft falls as cumulative output increases and Boeing has over thirty years' experience of constructing 747 jumbo jets. And the company shares overhead costs and technology with military production for its largest single customer, the US government.

But although most of the aircraft you see at Heathrow or Kennedy are Boeings, that reflects the past rather than the present or future. Airbus has won an increasing share of the market and today the European company has larger orders and more exciting new aircraft.

My account failed to recognise another key factor. Sustained dominance depends on complete commitment to a market and to market leadership. The commitment that once characterised IBM and today characterises Microsoft. The commitment you see at Philip Morris, Coca-Cola, or Disney. These companies' first priority is to win, to beat the competition, and profits are the satisfactory result rather than the primary concern.

Boeing was once the archetype of such businesses. Bill Boeing was an engineer who loved aircraft. But the architect of the modern company was a lawyer, Bill Allen, chief executive from 1945. For Allen 'Boeing is always reaching out for tomorrow. This can only be accomplished by people who live, breathe, eat and sleep what they are doing.' When a non-executive director, Crawford Greenwalt, asked for information about expected returns from the 747, Boeing's largest and riskiest project, he was rebuffed. Robert Sperling, in his history of Boeing, writes 'Greenwalt just put his head down on the table and muttered "My God, these guys don't even know what the return-on-investment will be on this thing." '

Boeing bet the company on the 747, and it was a close run thing. The first model was delivered to Pan Am in 1969 but the aviation market was shaken by the oil shock of the early 1970s. But later in the decade world airlines resumed growth. With little competition to the 747 thereafter, very little discounting was needed to keep selling. We still don't know what the return-on-investment was, but it was probably very large.

In the mid 1990s, Boeing acquired McDonnell Douglas and a new management team led by Harry Stonecipher and Phil Condit. Condit proudly talked of taking the company into 'a value based environment where unit cost, return on investment, shareholder return are the measures by which you'll be judged'.*

Boeing's recent strategy reflected that approach: increasingly sceptical of large investment in new aircraft, dropping plans for a sonic cruiser and a stretched jumbo jet. The company's focus has been on meeting the growing needs of the US military. Airbus, like the old Boeing company, was about aircraft first and money second: it came into being as technological flagship rather than commercial venture. But, as for Boeing, planes turned into profit.

We will never know whether Boeing could have made more

money for its shareholders with a different approach. In an uncertain world the prospective ROI on the 747 could never have been meaningfully calculated. But we do know that Condit's refocusing of Boeing was unsuccessful in its own terms – the stock price when he resigned was 20% lower than when he was appointed. And we do know I was mistaken when I told classes that Europe could never regain supremacy in civil aircraft manufacture.

---

* In *Business Week*, 7 April 1998

Business heroes

SUN TZU

4 AUGUST 1999

Sun Tzu (approx. 500 BC) may or may not have existed, and
if he did exist may or may not have written *The Art of War*, the
work attributed to him. The complex and confusing history
is described in Dr Lionel Giles' introduction to the scholarly
(1910) English translation of this ancient Chinese text. The
book was known in military circles in Korea and Japan as well as
in China and was popularised in the 1980s by the novelist James
Clavell. This reprint coincided with growing interest in business
circles in the economic development of these countries.

The *Financial Times* finds it difficult to celebrate summer. It is faced with thinness of events, editorial material and advertising, and readers with time on their hands. So it is offering a serialisation of business classics.

Where else to begin but with the oldest work on strategy – Sun Tzu's *The Art of War*. It is fashionable today to argue that what we knew last year, or last week, is already out of date. But also fashionable to look much further back in time. To people who could not conceivably have envisaged any of the business situations we face today – Adam Smith, Machiavelli, and Sun Tzu. Military strategists must have lessons for modern executives. After all, it's a battlefield out there.

The military analogy has a powerful hold on business thinking. The very term strategy is a direct acknowledgement of this. And yet the analogy is profoundly misleading. We talk of the Cola Wars – the competitive jockeying between Coke and Pepsi which has taken place over decades and around the world. Similar 'battles' take place in many other industries. Yet there is an obvious difference between the Cola Wars and the war in Kosovo, or the great world wars of this century.

In military conflicts the object is to inflict damage on the enemy until, unable to tolerate such damage further, one protagonist gives way to the wishes of the other. The two players in the Cola Wars, however, have continued to be successful and prosperous companies. The more vigorous the 'war' the better both have done. Rivalry between them has expanded the market and stimulated their efficiency and resourcefulness in ways that have benefited both their customers and the companies themselves. In all probability the 'wars' will continue for ever. Not in Pepsi's wildest fantasies does it imagine that the conflict will end in a second burning of Atlanta.

Military conflict is about mutual destruction, and generally ends in defeat or exhaustion, which is why the scale of resources available to each side is crucial. Business competition is rarely of this kind. There need be no fundamental inconsistency between the objectives of the different players. And business competition is usually of indefinite duration.

Occasionally business situations do have some of the characteristics of military conflict. There are battles to establish market standards, as with Microsoft's dominance of the PC market with MS-DOS and Windows, or JVC's success with VHS in the video-recorder business. These do have a single victor and conclude when the defeated party withdraws. But even here the analogy is far from exact. Direct damage to the other side, even if legal, is rarely an important or effective tactic. And such standard wars are particular and unusual. In the main, business competition works to everyone's long run benefit, which is why sensible public policy is in favour of business competition and against military conflict.

★ ★ ★

Still, the military analogy retains a powerful hold on our thinking. Boys in business, deprived of other outlets for their aggression, vent it in memos about competitors. Sometimes these end up in the hands of anti-trust authorities. Perhaps the arrival of more women in the boardroom will change this. But the evidence so far is not encouraging. As with the first women soldiers, some female executives seem to feel a need to prove themselves with equally vigorous assertion of a macho culture (see p.92).

It is easy to see why the image of the CEO as commander-in-chief appeals to many who hold, or aspire to, these positions. It is satisfying to think that one's detailed strategy will be translated into action by platoons trained and disciplined to unthinking obedience. But the distance between plans drawn in the war room and experience in the trenches is reproduced in many corporations.

And the military analogy is often in the minds of those who believe that size is the main, or only, source of competitive advantage in business. Yet here most of all military conflict and business competition differ. The outcome of the Second World War was inevitable because of the magnitude of the resources that the United States and Soviet Union were able to bring to bear. If business had similar characteristics, the rise and fall of great corporations would be like the rise and fall of great powers – a matter of centuries rather than, as we have learnt, a matter of a few years. In war, resources lead to success: in business, success leads to resources. This is a fundamental difference between the processes of war and competition.

It was not always so. Once, military adventures were often designed to obtain more resources to fight more wars. Once, business development depended on the favours of already rich men. This was the world in which Sun Tzu lived. But, in the twentieth century, the relevance of established resources to military success was reinforced, while the relevance of established resources to business success was diminished. In the century of total war states were, for the first time in history, able to mobilise the whole of their population and their economies in support of their military objectives. In the century of expanding capital markets, anyone with a sufficiently good idea could attract the resources to establish a business.

And yet Sun Tzu's teachings still have relevance for us today. Sun Tzu understood that the most successful battles are those you do not actually fight. Modern business people obsessed by military analogies would do well to remember that.

Corporation of the century

22 DECEMBER 1999

As we gather round the digital Christmas tree, it is time to choose the corporate personality of the century. As with any Christmas game, I must first explain the rules. When I talk of corporate personality, I mean just that: the company, not the individual. The law created the concept of corporate personality over a century ago, distinguishing the company from the individuals who run it, own its shares, or work for it. I think corporate personality is a useful idea, as a commercial as well as legal feature of successful companies. The modern tendency to equate the actions of the firm with the ideas of the chief executive leads us to miss important features of what makes these companies successful.

And I decided, reluctantly, to confine the competition to the century rather than the millennium. The most serious contender from outside the twentieth century is the East India Company, which founded an empire and established the modern international trading system. Still, Robert Clive and Warren Hastings are no longer around to receive their awards, and I do not think the chief executives of the states of India and Bangladesh would willingly see themselves as their successors.

For related reasons, the company which most computer junkies would choose, the one that literally stares them in the face, did not make it to the final list. True, Microsoft now has the largest market capitalisation of any company in the world. But that market capitalisation far exceeds any revenues or profits it has earned in the twentieth century. The valuation of Microsoft shares is the product not of its achievement in the twentieth century, but of the expectation that this provides a platform for far greater achievement in the twenty-first. So Bill Gates will have to wait for his Oscar.

The car had the impact in the twentieth century that internet enthusiasts claim information technology will have in the twenty-first. The availability of cheap, efficient personal transport changed everyday life and the opportunity to deliver goods quickly, reliably and flexibly had an impact on every aspect of business life. Most of my short list were direct or indirect beneficiaries of the development of the automobile.

Ford and General Motors are both strong contenders. Anyone writing in 1900, and correctly foreseeing the impact of the automobile, would nevertheless have stood no chance at all of identifying Ford and General Motors as the companies to watch. These companies are there not just because they led the transport revolution. Ford invented mass production and General Motors the modern divisionalised corporation. In doing so, they influenced every other business.

The car also accounts for the success of non–American companies among the finalists. Shell is unquestionably European corporate personality of the century. Yet while an extraordinary performer in its own right – it is almost the only business to have maintained the same degree of dominance in every decade of the century – it does not seem to have had the exemplary effect on the management of other businesses that would qualify it for the top spot.

Toyota certainly has had such an effect. The company not only symbolises Japanese success in creating and dominating a world market in durable goods. It forced even the most monolithic of American firms – such as the late century General Motors – to rethink the ways in which they organised their activities. Yet, in Japanese style, no one Japanese company stands out overwhelmingly from its compatriots. Japan Inc. might win, but not any single Japanese firm.

The twentieth century was above all the century of the large manufacturing corporation. Some of these, like Ford and General Motors, were distinguished for the creation and management of operations of hitherto unimagined complexity. Shell, although not a manufacturing business, did the same. But another group of successful manufacturers were those who exploited the possibilities established by national transport and national media to develop an entirely modern business – the provision of branded fast-moving consumer goods.

Procter and Gamble, Unilever, Philip Morris and Coca-Cola are names to conjure with here. It is a measure of how much business has changed that the modern marketing we associate with these companies had barely been invented a century ago.

I tried, but failed, to find a retailer or a financial services business which deserved to make the final short list. Sears Roebuck seemed too old, Wal-Mart too new. The life cycle of the successful retailer seems so short that such companies cannot do well in a competition where prolonged records of success are essential.

And no bank seemed to have a strong enough claim. J. P. Morgan and Goldman Sachs had powerful corporate personalities, but they are hardly the businesses of the century. Perhaps American regulatory restrictions on financial institutions prevented any company achieving the position in the banking industry which General Motors, or Microsoft, or Procter and Gamble achieved in theirs. Perhaps banking management had – maybe still has – an unparalleled ability to screw up its own business even as it advises others how to run theirs.

But there is a clear winner. One company dominates its businesses at the end of the century as it dominated its – different – businesses a hundred years ago. It has always been one of the world's most admired companies – whatever its activities. Its chief executive – whoever he has been – has always been one of the world's most admired businessmen. It has led every innovation in management thinking – and followed every fad. Step forward General Electric, corporate personality of the century.

Microsoft's position as the company with the largest market capitalisation proved to be a transitory phenomenon of the dot.com bubble. As the bubble subsided, it lost that position to – General Electric.

Business heroes

JACK WELCH

31ST OCTOBER 2001

Jack Welch (1935 –) joined General Electric in 1960 after
completing a PhD in chemical engineering at the University of
Illinois. He rose rapidly through the company being Chairman
and CEO in 1981, retiring in 2001 with a well established
position as America's most admired businessman. His reputation
was somewhat tarnished when, after an affair with the then editor
of *Harvard Business Review* (now his wife), divorce proceedings
revealed details of his extravagant post-retirement perquisites from
the company he had headed with such distinction.

A friend has finally, at the age of 50, learned to swim. It took him that long to find a good swimming teacher. Swimming teachers are usually good swimmers. But the very factors that make such people good swimmers make them bad teachers. They have an affinity for water and do not understand the problem of bad swimmers, who don't.

That is why the skills of the swimmer are not the same as the skills of the swimming teacher. For the same reason, business biographies and autobiographies are not the same as management textbooks. Anyone who buys Jack Welch's book hoping to learn how to run a business has gone to the wrong shelf of the business bookshop.

Alfred Sloan's *My Years with General Motors* is the only business autobiography which might be found on a reading list in a serious business school or university – and one of the very few still in print decades after the death of its author. But Sloan's is a highly unusual autobiography. It tries to exclude any personal information about its author. Sloan was a rigorously intellectual figure, generally regarded as the inventor of the modern divisionalised corporation. He set out to write a management text.

The writing of Sloan's arch-rival, Henry Ford, is very different. Ford wrote to disseminate what he imagined to be important insights on the iniquities of the Federal Government, the immorality of tobacco, and the machinations of Jews.

The things we learn from such books are rarely the things their authors intend. Ford's autobiography tells us that Henry, although a business genius and the inspired founder of a great corporation, became an unpleasant bigot ill equipped to run the huge company which bore his name. From *Losing my Virginity*, we learn that Richard Branson is an able self-publicist. From Lee Iacocca we learn that there are no bounds to human vanity.

Jack Welch's autobiography contrasts with these self-serving tomes. The Welch who emerges is an attractive and engaging figure. There is a lot about golf.

The features of good management that Welch emphasises contain nothing original; integrity and openness in discussion; concern to build committed teams by careful selection and deselection of members; an approach to problem-solving that is rational and analytic yet decisive. However cynical you feel about the reality of GE, it says much for Welch that these are the attributes of management style that he regards as important. The overall picture is of a man whom you would like to have as your boss. The real management lesson of Welch's book is that a great chief executive of a great corporation is a person whom other talented managers would like to work for.

But it is not what happens. When you finish reading the memoirs of Ford, or Iacocca, you do so with a sense of relief that you have never been their immediate subordinate. No able person could enjoy working for anyone with such an overwhelming sense of their own rightness. Such leaders find themselves surrounded by second-rate sycophants. Henry Ford ended his career able to confide only in his security chief.

Ford's very success made him a bad developer of management talent. Success took its toll on Welch too: as time and his book go on his reports of decision making become ever more personalised. Welch's account of his dealings with the European Commission over Honeywell is unintentionally comic.

The most important characteristic of a good boss of a large organisation is good assistants. Only such leadership can sustain long-term success for the business, as it has done for GE. Welch describes the daunting task of succeeding Reg Jones, who was then the most admired chief executive in America (as Ralph Cordiner had been before him). It is very likely that Jeff Immelt's successor will face the same problem. It is to GE, rather than to Jack Welch, that we should look for management lessons.

Stake the territory

In which the first are sometimes last,
and the last sometimes first.

Positioning is key

20 JANUARY 1999

English retailing is like English gardening. In the background there are hardy perennials – Marks & Spencer, John Lewis, J. Sainsbury, Harrods. They remain, sturdy and reliable for decades. In front the annuals flourish briefly and then fade. Sock shops, branches of Laura Ashley. Coffee shops are opening everywhere. But the hot bread shops have vanished like melting snow, and Next Interiors is no more. Sometimes, like Next, old plants flower again on different stems.

Last week, one of the most reliable of the perennials, Marks & Spencer, revealed signs of ill-health. Sears, owner of Selfridges and enough shoe shops to satisfy Imelda Marcos, is about to be pruned, thinned and even dug up by the roots. What do we know about retail horticulture? What makes retailers flourish? What distinguishes annuals from perennials? Are some of our perennials in need of renewal?

Short-term competitive advantages in retailing are often derived from novel positioning. George Davies, who developed Next, saw that there was a market for stylish clothing for a slightly older age group of women than those targeted by fashion retailers. Body Shop, Direct Line and pubs with real ales and no loud music were all the results of similar insight into unmet needs.

But once recognised, needs are rarely unmet for long. The niche Davies had identified was rapidly invaded by competitors, many of them with stronger retailing skills. At the same time, the company persuaded itself that its success was the result, not of transitory dominance of a neglected market segment, but of a universal management genius applicable to a wide range of retail activities. Next went on a spree of acquisition and diversification, and came close to nemesis as a result.

These errors are easy to identify with hindsight. But not easy enough for Ratners, which made almost exactly the same mistakes nearly a decade later. Gerald Ratner recognised a market for low cost, low quality jewellery. But as his success became evident, others could sell the same products, and did. Ratner also began a programme of acquisition; but all the company could bring to the business it bought was the no-longer-original concept of selling cheap goods. Ratner's accurate denigration of his own products (he resigned after publicly describing them as crap) only hastened the outcome which the weakness of the underlying strategy made inevitable.

Positioning is not a source of sustainable competitive advantage for any business, because competitive advantage based on positioning alone is readily replicable. For a time, one British retailer – Kwik Save – seemed to be an exception to this rule. For several years it earned one of the highest returns on capital employed of any large British company. But the formula – branded goods sold at low prices in unattractive surroundings in secondary locations – was based on positioning, and readily reproducible positioning at that.

But, in the consumer boom of the 1980s, it was not reproduced. The flight to quality was a business cliché of the time. Kwik Save's natural competitors, Gateway and Asda,* moved up-market in unsuccessful emulation of Sainsbury and Tesco. Recession, and entry by continental discounters such as Aldi and Netto, eventually proved that Kwik Save was indeed no exception to the basic rule that positioning is not enough. The profits vanished, and soon after, so did the company.

Asda and Gateway hoped to match the repositioning accomplished a decade earlier by Tesco. That company's early success was based, like Kwik Save's, on positioning: 'pile 'em high; sell 'em cheap' had been the slogan of Jack Cohen, the company's founder, in an era in which the abolition of price maintenance by manufacturers in 1964 had enabled food retailers for the first time to base their strategy on aggressive price competition.

But a decade later, a new generation of Tesco's managers recognised that positioning was imitable. So their market was under threat, as Kwik Save's would be, while the growing strengths of the company's systems enabled it to compete effectively in mainstream food retailing. Abruptly, in 1976, the company repositioned itself, in direct competition with market leader Sainsbury. The shift was a substantial gamble, and a triumphant success: over the following two decades Tesco would become the UK's largest retailer. Positioning matched competitive advantage: but positioning was not the underlying source of competitive advantage.

As Marks & Spencer itself would illustrate. The company's traditional strength was in clothing, where its competitive advantage was based on the distinctive capabilities derived from those and detailed management of supplier relationships and the reputation it enjoyed with customers. Most diversifications, such as that with household goods, enjoyed little success, with one exception: food. Those close partnerships with manufacturers which had translated Marks & Spencer's knowledge of its customers into successful products proved to work best, not in the mid-market segment where the company's clothing was so successful, but at the top of the food retailing market, where Marks & Spencer created an entirely new quality image for manufactured food. The company came to recognise two different customer bases (and would, in the long run, dedicate many of its stores to one or other product group). Different positionings matched the same distinctive capability in different product markets.

How that distinctive capability would be lost is another story (p.76).

---

* Asda would be acquired in 1999 by Wal-Mart while Gateway (now known as Somerfield) went through successive, and largely unproductive, rounds of rebranding.

First movers please

13 MAY 1998

Do you remember Berkey or Ampex? Gablinger or Chux? Product innovators all. Berkey produced the first hand-held electronic calculators, Ampex the first video recorders, Gablinger developed the first low alcohol lagers, Chux sold the first disposable nappies.

But none of these companies made a sustained commercial success of their innovations. Today the calculators we use are probably made by Casio, our video recorder comes from Matsushita: our low alcohol beer is Philip Morris's Miller Lite,* the diapers we buy are made by Procter and Gamble. The pioneer was swept away.

EMI has one of the most remarkable records in innovation of any company – a first in television, and computers, its CAT scanner transformed radiography. But EMI has not made any of these products for many years.† Today televisions come from Sony, computers from IBM or Dell, and GE is market leader in scanners.

Xerox established the photocopier market, and even if its dominance was ultimately challenged by Canon it remains a large and successful company today. But Xerox was also a pioneer in fax machines and personal computers. Each product proved to be a major success – but not for Xerox.

Apple developed the personal computer market. But IBM would create the products we all use today. Still, Apple then jumped ahead once more by introducing the graphical user interface. Icons and mice brought personal computing within the reach of people who did not know how to program a computer. But Microsoft's Windows would be the means through which the world gained access to computers. The business environment is often unkind to technological pioneers.

The failures of EMI may be contrasted with the success of Glaxo, a pharmaceutical company which emerged from relative obscurity to be one of Britain's most successful businesses. Both companies had, in the 1970s, a product which would ultimately take the US health care market by storm. CAT scanners and anti-ulcerants were both to win Nobel prizes for the British scientists who invented them.

But there the similarities end. EMI was proud to employ Geoffrey Houndsfield, who invented the scanner. The company established a US distribution network and manufacturing facility to exploit his innovation. But it was quickly crushed by the superior political, marketing and technical skills of GE.

The prize for anti-ulcerants went to James Black. But Black did not work for Glaxo, but for its then competitor Smith Kline. Glaxo's Zantac was an imitative product, second to market, developed through refocusing of that company's research after Black's discovery. US distribution was initially contracted to Hoffman la Roche, the only foreign-owned drug company previously to have enjoyed major success in US distribution. The superior marketing skills of Glaxo and its partners enabled Zantac to overtake Smith Kline's Tagamet and become the world's best selling drug. Glaxo's achievement was based not on the speed or quality of the company's innovation but on its commercial skills in exploiting that innovation.

If technological innovation is frequently imitated, it is generally even easier to follow innovations in business process. Direct Line (which pioneered directly sold insurance) is inevitably and predictably losing market share to established insurers. American Express pioneered plastic money, but Citibank, Bank of America and even Sears would capture the market with Mastercard, Visa and Discover. Innovative positioning is even more easily replicated – Next and Ratners identified unexploited market niches only to find that established retailers could do the same job at least as well.

Why do so many people in business emphasise first mover

advantages? Sometimes, we use hindsight to describe the successful adopter as the first mover. Lotus became dominant in spreadsheets not because it was the first or the best but because it was the product available at the moment the market was ready to take off.** Even if you know how a market will develop, timing is a matter of luck – or of quite exceptional skill.

There are people of great originality who use these attributes to build great businesses. General Electric was built on the extraordinary fecundity of Thomas Edison's mind, the Ford Motor company on the abilities of its eponymous founder. The imagination of Walt Disney created a company which is still without parallel or rival. Akio Morita of Sony occupies a similar place in the annals of modern business. However, while many chief executives may see themselves as Edisons, or Fords, Disneys or Moritas, not many actually are. Genius is indeed a source of competitive advantage, but necessarily a rare one.

The success of large established corporations – Matsushita, Philip Morris, IBM or General Electric – is generally based on other things: their distribution capability, their depth of technical expertise, their marketing skills. Time and again these characteristics enable them to develop the original concept far more effectively than the originators themselves.

When you are told that the key to the future business success is to see the future more quickly or more clearly than other people, ask which established cases in business history illustrate the point. And try to remember Berkey and Ampex, Gablinger and Chux.

---

* Miller, a long established US brewing company, was acquired in 1969 by tobacco company Philip Morris. Miller Lite was launched in 1986. In 2002 Philip Morris (now Altria) sold Miller to South African Breweries.

† After many mergers and demergers, EMI today is a music publishing business.

** Lotus 1-2-3 quickly became the market leading spreadsheet after the launch of the IBM PC. In the 1990s, Lotus 1-2-3 was in turn overtaken by Microsoft's Excel.

Innovate or die

13 OCTOBER 1999

Akio Morita, one of the founders of the Sony Corporation, died two weeks ago. His love of publicity and Manhattan socialising made him the first, and still almost the only, Japanese business leader to be well known outside his native country. His company has entered the Western imagination more completely than any other Japanese business.

What was the secret of Sony's success? The history of the company is full of lessons about competitive advantage in business. The corporation's founding prospectus proclaimed that the purpose of incorporation was 'creating an ideal workplace, free, dynamic and joyous, where dedicated engineers will be able to realise their craft and skills at the highest possible level' and goes on to assert 'we shall eliminate any untoward profit-seeking, shall constantly emphasise activities of real substance, and shall not seek expansion of size for the sake of size.'

Since we are often told today that no institutional investor would want to invest in a company with aims like that, it is worth recording that an early buyer of Sony stock would have become exceedingly rich – the Morita foundation's stake in the company is today worth more than $5bn. Nor would such an investor necessarily have done better if the firm's objective had been to maximise shareholder value through growth from a programme of strategic acquisitions. Morita's flirtation with Wall Street led to Sony's principal acquisition and greatest debacle, the purchase of Columbia studios.

Sony's organic growth was based on technology-based product innovation – transistor radios that would fit in a pocket, televisions with true-to-life colours, the ubiquitous walkman, the compact disc, the playstation. Yet innovation as such is rarely a sustainable source of competitive advantage.

Sony's leap to greatness came through its development of the transistor radio, using a licence bought from Bell Laboratories for $25,000. Even this advance then seemed a lot of money to a company and a government short of foreign exchange: but it secured access to probably the most important invention ever made in a commercial research establishment. The transistor made almost no money for AT&T, which owned Bell Labs. The underlying physics was in the public domain, and the practicalities of commercial development and the particularities of the parent company's market dominance dictated a generous licensing strategy. The benefits of fundamental innovation are difficult to appropriate. If Bell Labs had been a purely commercial venture, rather than the technological flagship of a huge telephone monopoly, it would probably not have been carrying out such research at all.

Sony learnt for itself the difficulty of appropriating the benefits of innovation when the company sought to maintain exclusivity in the Betamax standard for video recorders. This strategy was comprehensively defeated by JVC, which preferred open licensing for its VHS system. Sony did not repeat this mistake with compact discs – where it generously conceded a half share in the outcome to its rival Philips, and licensed the standard freely. The Walkman, an innovation so simple that once seen, it can be reproduced by anyone, could not be protected: yet Sony continued to be a market-leading supplier. The source of competitive advantage was not the result of the innovation in itself.

Competitive advantage in innovative industries is rarely the product of the quality of innovation, and this is not how Sony became one of the world's great companies or Morita one of the world's great businessmen. Sony's competitive advantage has been based on two factors: the establishment of an environment that produces an endless stream of consumer oriented innovations, and the development of complementary skills and assets – the first Japanese brand to fire the imagination of consumers – which secures ready acceptance of these innovations in the market place.

It is usually wrong to personalise the achievements of businesses, but broadly we could associate Sony's innovative environment with Morita's founding partner, Masaru Ibuka, and the company's marketing flair with Morita himself. Ibuka wrote the founding prospectus and created the joyous environment that produced not only joy and Nobel prizes for Sony engineers but also great joy and wealth for Sony distributors, customers and shareholders. Morita made shirts with larger pockets so that his transistor radios were truly pocketable, saw the need for an international brand for a Japanese company, and understood the overwhelming importance of the US consumer market.

Commercial success in innovation markets depends crucially on the other attributes a firm brings to the process of developing and marketing innovation. That is why Japanese firms, Sony pre-eminent among them, have outdistanced their European and American rivals in consumer electronics. And why Sony's purchase of a film studio was an absurd diversion from its real competitive strengths.

Define your business expansively

1 DECEMBER 1995

Granada's bid for Forte is an audacious attempt to create Britain's largest leisure business – one that would stretch from Coronation Street to the Savoy Hotel, from Newport Pagnell service area to television rentals. But is there such a thing as a leisure business? Or just a range of things people do with their spare time?

In the last decade, many companies have posed the question 'what business are we in?' The intellectual spur came from a series of articles by Ted Levitt, the American marketing guru behind Maurice Saatchi's aspirations to create a global advertising business.

Levitt blasted companies for what he described as 'marketing myopia'. Railroads had gone into terminal decline, but only because they had limited their horizons to the tracks. Neither people nor goods had stopped moving. If only railroads had seen themselves as being in the transportation business – if they had been customer-led rather than product-led – they might still be prosperous. Levitt acknowledged that no product improvement could have saved the buggy whip industry from Henry Ford's model T. But if the buggy whip people had appreciated that they too were in the transportation business, they might have survived as makers of fan belts or air filters.

Levitt's analysis of the petroleum industry was particularly forceful. Firms like Exxon and Amoco, BP and Shell had long laboured under the misapprehension that they were oil companies. Levitt told them they were in the energy business. If they continued to confine their attention to oil and gasoline, they risked going the way of the buggy whip manufacturers.

His advice was influential. Oil companies, fearful after the 1974 oil shock, did buy coal mines and diversify into other energy markets. The results ranged from disappointing to disastrous. Few of these activities survive. The major oil companies continue to make their considerable profits out of selling oil.

The Levitt thesis is fundamentally misconceived. The term business – as used in the question 'what business are we in?' – conflates two distinct economic concepts – the market and the industry. The market is defined by consumer needs and reflects consumer demands. The industry is defined by related firm capabilities and supply technologies.

So washing machines and laundries are in the same market, because both are means of cleaning clothes. Washing machines and refrigerators are products of the same industry, despite their different purposes, because each is a white box with a motor sold through similar distribution channels. Confusing the industry with the market is one of the most frequently repeated mistakes in corporate strategy.

There was an energy market – coal and oil served similar purposes. But no energy industry – the skills needed to dig coal are different from those needed to manage an integrated oil company, as firms which tried to do both discovered. Penn Central could have taken to the skies, and the buggy whip manufacturers might have made air filters, but there is no reason to think that they would have been any good at these activities: no reason to think that they would have performed better than any other firm which saw airlines or automobile components as a new market opportunity.

The examples Levitt used to make his case demonstrated his error. At the time he wrote DuPont and Corning had indeed continued to succeed in the nylon and glass businesses. But they had not done it by diversifying into substitutes like cotton or tinplate. What they had done was to find new uses for their core products and key skills. Levitt had simply confused the evolution of an industry with the evolution of a market.

So how should a firm define its core business? Is BT in the

integrated provision of telecommunications products (as it once thought when it bought Mitel, a hardware supplier)? Or in the international provision of telecommunications services (as it next thought when it bought McCaw, an American cellular phone company)? Or in the business of global data transmission for multi-channels (the rationale of its current alliance with MCI)? Or just a phone company? (see p. 112)

The way to resolve these questions is not by necessarily inconclusive debate on whether buggy whips are instruments of correction or transportation accessories. Even if that question could be resolved, it would not tell their manufacturers whether to diversify into thumbscrews or motor cars. The right approach is to identify what are the distinctive skills and capabilities of the firm and the markets in which these yield competitive advantage.

Posing the question that way shows why it was right for DuPont to seek out new uses for polyester fibres, but wrong for oil companies to buy coal mines. It shows why it was right for Marks & Spencer to diversify into financial services (because that capitalised on its reputation with customers) but wrong for BT to own an equipment manufacturer.

And why there is no such thing as the leisure business. We have heard about the leisure business before – from Rank when it attempted to buy Watneys, from Bass when it mistakenly acquired Horizon Holidays. Package tours and an evening in the pub may represent alternative claims on consumer expenditure, but that does not mean that there is a leisure industry of which both are part. Firms should always ask whether a new activity extends the application of their distinctive capabilities? If it does not, it is no more your business than it is anyone else's.

Granada succeeded in taking over Forte and creating Britain's largest leisure business. Over the subsequent decade, it disposed of all the activities it had purchased in this transaction, and its own diversified leisure activities, retreating to its base in television and finally merging with Carlton to form the dominant commercial broadcaster in the UK.

Envision the future

30 AUGUST 1996

Competing for the Future, by Gary Hamel and C. K. Prahalad, has been one of the best selling business books of the last year. The authors argue that changes in technology, and the growth of international competition, mean that traditional boundaries between different markets and between different industries are eroding. The firms that survive into the next century will be those that first perceive these changes, and act accordingly.

It is easy to understand why this thesis is seductive. The claim that the only constraints on our success are the limits of our imagination, although generally false, has lifted hearts for millennia. Grand visions take precedence over prosaic numbers. And since the search for vision makes acquisitions and alliances central items on every company's agenda, an army of advisers is waiting to applaud and assist.

So SmithKline Beecham is redefining pharmaceuticals as the health care business. Scottish Power knows that the future lies with multi-utilities. Media companies are exploring their versions of convergence. 'The challenge is to pierce the fog of uncertainty and develop great foresight into the whereabouts of tomorrow's markets'. Every business needs to contemplate different customers, different markets, different products, different technologies. The specific assertion of Prahalad and Hamel (PH) is that future business success will largely be based on early identification of changes in the boundaries of markets and industries. 'Some management teams were simply more 'foresightful' than others. Some were capable of imagining products, services, and entire industries that did not yet exist and then giving them birth'. (p xi)

But there are good reasons for scepticism about the degree to which such foresightfulness is the basis of competitive advantage. AT&T correctly predicted the convergence of computing and communications, but was mistaken in believing that this should be the basis of its business organisation. Xerox demonstrated foresight in recognising that the personal computer and the fax machine would be important new products in the 1980s but failed to make money out of either innovation. The oil companies who diversified into coal and minerals in the 1970s under the influence of an earlier version of the envision the future thesis – Levitt's 'marketing myopia' preceded PH's 'product myopia' by around 20 years – lived to regret their purchases.

So what evidence do PH present for their claims? As is often the case with business fashions, the main evidence for the effectiveness of the treatment is the number and prestige of the other patients who are taking it. PH identify eight companies which have prospered by 'reinventing their industry'. Merck has integrated forward into managed health care. British Airways seeks to become the world's first truly global airline. Bell Atlantic has a vision of an integrated infocommunications company. But it may be premature to claim success for these 'reinventions'. Bell Atlantic's diversification into infocommunications has now been sidelined in favour of just becoming a bigger phone company by merger with Nynex. British Airways, nursing heavy losses on its investments in US Air and Qantas, now seeks to double its bets through an alliance with American Airlines. And the benefits of Merck's costly purchase of Medco are still to be demonstrated.

Then there are two firms, ISS and Service Corporation, which have pioneered international acquisitions in industries – contract cleaning and funerals – where the benefits of global organisation are not, at first glance, obvious. They are not more obvious at second or third glance: and it now appears that the financial record of ISS owes less to the reinvention of its business than the reinvention of its accounts.

The three other inclusions on PH's list do not seem to have much to do with their argument. Wal-Mart and Hewlett Packard are undeniably successful companies, but their success seems to be based on doing, very well, very similar things to their competitors. And CNN is a fine example of inspired identification of a market opportunity, superbly executed. Yet what industry did CNN reinvent?

It is easier to find examples of firms whose attempts to redefine their industry were costly failures than ones which used them to establish sustainable competitive advantage: Citibank's repeatedly unsuccessful strategy of establishing pan-European retail banking; the attempt through the Alleghis Corporation to integrate United Airlines into a 'total travel experience'; Saatchi and Saatchi's creation of a global advertising business.

And we should not be surprised by this. Anticipating the evolution of markets and industries is hard, and even if a firm picks the direction correctly the timing is a matter of fine judgment. Citibank and Saatchi were wrong in the 1980s, but one day their strategic assessment will probably be right. The advantages of being first are rarely so decisive that they clearly outweigh the risks of being wrong, or simply premature. It is not the people which pioneered jet aircraft or pocket calculators, superstores or personal computers, video recorders or junk bond financing, package holidays or fax machines, who are market leaders today. Genuine foresight was rapidly overtaken by other companies. Boeing and Casio, Sainsbury and IBM, Matsushita and Salomon, Thomson and Canon had real competitive advantages based on the only sustainable source of competitive advantage – a distinctive capability unmatched and unmatchable by rivals.

The problem – as so often in the frenzied world of business publishing – is that entirely sensible, if limited, advice is turned into misleading prescription by crass hyperbole. Every company should be alive to changes in the nature of its markets, the needs of its customers, and the opportunities which are presented by new technology. But overestimation of the impact of these changes on competitive positions, and an exaggerated view of the imminence of radical change in industry structure, has led far too many firms into ill considered acquisitions. The direct and indirect costs of acquisitions are high and mistakes are seldom easily or cheaply reversible. Do not be too ready to accept that 'new competitive realities have ruptured industry boundaries, overthrown much of standard management practice, and rendered conventional models of strategy and growth obsolete'. They have not.

Back to the future

JANUARY 2006

The twelve companies commended by C. K. Prahalad and Gary Hamel (PH) in *Competing for the Future* enjoyed mixed fortunes in the decade that followed. Four were singled out for 'reinventing their industries'. Wal-Mart goes on from strength to strength; CNN is now part of the Time-Warner media conglomerate; ISS and Service Corporation, businesses much hyped in the 1990s by analysts as well as gurus, never regained reputations tainted by scandals and controversy.

Four companies were applauded for the success with which they 'regenerated their strategy'. All performed poorly and were acquired by larger companies in the same industry: AT&T, Compaq, JPMorgan and Bankers Trust were folded into SBC, Hewlett Packard, Chase, and Deutsche Bank respectively.

The diversification efforts which were commended as representing both 'reinvention of their industry' and 'regeneration of their strategy' were subsequently unwound at Merck, which disposed of its distribution business, Medis, in 2003, at British Airways, which abandoned its policy of buying strategic stakes in other airlines, and at Bell Atlantic, now Verizon, predominantly a telecoms company rather than an infocommunications business. Hewlett Packard hired the colourful Carly Fiorina to revive its fortunes, and acquired Compaq: events discussed further at p. 93.

Peters and Waterman, whose 1982 book *In Search of Excellence* was a business blockbuster a decade before PH, were criticised when some of their 'excellent' companies such as Atari and Wang subsequently failed (although a *Fortune* survey two decades later showed that the group as a whole had continued substantial outperformance). But this response is largely unjustified. The competitive advantage of once excellent companies may erode, either as a result of decline in their own distinctive capabilities or of changes in the business environment in which they operate. Characteristics which made particular businesses outstanding when Peters and Waterman wrote may not be appropriate, or sustained, at a different time. My own *Foundations of Corporate Success* contains admiring references to Marks & Spencer, identifying competitive advantages which the company lost in the 1990s (see p. 76). Subsequent events do not invalidate, perhaps even reinforce, the original argument.

But the present case is different. The PH book was entitled *Competing for the Future*: its central thesis was, in the authors' own words, 'a view of strategy that recognises it is not enough to optimally position a company with existing markets; the challenge is to pierce the fog of uncertainty and develop great foresight into the whereabouts of tomorrow's markets … a view of strategy that is less concerned with ensuring a tight fit between goals and resources and is more concerned with creating stretch goals that challenge employees to accomplish the seemingly impossible.'

The historical record suggests that these claims are simply not true. It is probable, indeed likely, that in due course there will be a small number of global airlines (although it is also likely that there will be a large number of locally based point-to-point carriers), and infocommunications is slowly becoming a reality. The companies exemplified by PH did not achieve exceptional success, or much success at all, by 'piercing the fog of uncertainty and developing great foresight into the whereabouts of tomorrow's markets': nor did 'challenging their employees to achieve the seemingly impossible' bring the impossible within reach. To the extent that blue sky thinking had any effect at all on the businesses in question, it led to ill-conceived diversification that was mostly reversed. Ensuring a 'tight fit between goals and resources' continues to be good advice.

The ego has landed

This was how the managers of one company whose chief executive would normally visit locations by helicopter to dispense opinion and instruction described the experience. The notion that large modern businesses depend on the extraordinary talents of exceptional individuals is persistently popular with business journalists, market analysts, and most of all with the individuals themselves. But it is not often supported by the experience of the companies in which they occupy elevated positions.

Search for excellence

26 MAY 1999

The world of business and economics often seems monochromatic. Marks & Spencer, once the epitome of all British business virtues, can now do nothing right. Much the same seems to have happened to Sainsbury's. General Motors was once America's most admired company, but no longer. The revolving door of fashion and favour went round rapidly for IBM – in, out, in once more

And the same is true of national economies. Barely two years ago Asian tigers were exemplars. Those who claimed at the beginning of the 1990s to see virtues in the German system of industrial organisation are today ridiculed. Business leaders are either heroes or villains. Watch out, Jack Welch and Richard Branson, for the revolving door.

When Peters and Waterman went *In Search of Excellence* in the 1980s, their approach was often interpreted in this way. Excellent companies did everything right, and the same was true of their leaders. You are either excellent, or not. 'Sculley – chump or champ?' screamed one business headline, struggling with the paradox that under John Sculley's stewardship Apple had enjoyed both periods of exceptional success and periods of abject failure. Disenchantment set in as some excellent companies didn't seem to be excellent any more. Peters and Waterman had classed Digital, Wang and Kmart as excellent.

Organisations and their leaders have both strengths and weaknesses. Sometimes times and markets are such that they allow the strengths to show through, and at other times they reflect the weaknesses. If An Wang and the company he founded were successful in one era and failed in another, that shows only that the capabilities of the corporation may be appropriate in one environment but inappropriate in another. If Sculley made some good judgments and some bad ones, that confirms that he is an ordinary human being, not a larger-than-life figure created by a business journalist. Apple's changing fortunes were the result of circumstances over which Sculley could have had little control even if he had been Thomas Edison, Henry Ford and Thomas Lipton rolled into one. Apple's development of the graphical user interface was in train before Sculley appeared on the scene, and there was nothing he could have done to prevent Microsoft developing a competitive product compatible with their own widely used operating system.

Organisations are similarly imperfect, and variously adapted to the circumstances they face. Ford once ruled the world car market with its model T, then General Motors overtook it, and Toyota then challenged General Motors. These companies succeeded not because they enjoyed some universal characteristic of excellence, but because they were, for a time, the right organisation for their market. We should not be surprised that they were the wrong organisation for their market at some different time. Microsoft came out ahead of IBM, not because Microsoft was more excellent than IBM, but because different phases of development of the computer market rewarded different capabilities.

The superficial, and common, reaction is to say that the truly excellent organisation is always successfully adapted to its time and market. But this is rarely possible. GE – perhaps the most successful corporation of the century – has reinvented itself several times. But that tells us that the competitive advantage of GE is quite special – a depth of management resource which seems effective in a very diverse range of activities. The distinctive capabilities of most companies – their brands, their reputations, their systems, their innovation abilities – are market- or product- specific.

So General Motors' competitive advantage simply and inevitably diminished as markets evolved in a direction less

.ole to its competitive advantages. GM could and did ,uire Toyota-like features but could never beat Toyota at Toyota's own game. IBM's success was in providing sales and support for large mainframe systems. Those competitive advantages simply could not be transferred to the PC business. The company goes on by redefining itself – less effectively – as a service company.

Corporations have characteristics and personalities like humans. Like humans, they can modify and change them but are unable to choose the personalities they want or require. Weaknesses are often related to strengths: determination is sometimes obstinacy, ambition is sometimes arrogance, inventiveness is sometimes unreliability, precision is sometimes bureaucracy.

That is why we are inclined to make black and white judgments about businesses as about people, and why these judgments are so often misleading. The sustained success of Marks & Spencer is an extraordinary testimony to the ability of organisational routines to extract exceptional performance from relatively ordinary people. These types of structure have always been effective at making incremental changes. The demand for improvement is ingrained: members of the company and its all embracing culture do not see such change as a threat. Such companies find discontinuous change much harder because of the need for organisational consensus.

So Marks & Spencer must change But its problem may be not that it must now change, but that it has already changed too much. The essence of that company's personality has been unswerving commitment to customer service, and sustained co-operative relationships with suppliers. Both of these have come under pressure in the cost-cutting environment of the 1990s. 'This above all – to thine own self be true/And it must follow, as the night the day,/ Thou canst not then be false to any man.' Personal, and corporate, success rests on establishing and defining one's own self.

There will be an answer

27 JUNE 1997

Standard Life and National Westminster are two businesses in the news. Each are organisations with a great past behind them. Each has a name which commands envy and respect. Each has well-publicised current problems. Although the two businesses and problems are very different, there is an important sense in which the issues they face are the same.

The banks central to the British economy in the twentieth century are products of the nineteenth. They came into existence to mobilise the small savings of individuals and lend them on to growing companies. Their effectiveness rested on the local knowledge of their managers, who were traditionally key figures in the local community. Their visibility gave confidence to depositors and allowed shrewd and informed assessments of the viability of the businesses the banks supported.

There were some advantages to scale in banking. National coverage gave depositors confidence in the stability of the institutions which they trusted with their savings. An institution with branches from Carlisle to Camborne seemed likely still to be there when savers wanted their money back. Marble banking halls and grandiose head offices reinforced the sense of permanence. And bigger banks were needed to handle bigger borrowers.

By the 1920s the number of major clearing banks in Britain was reduced to five. Midland, its roots in Britain's manufacturing heartland, was not just the largest bank in Britain; it was the largest bank in the world. Its rivals – Barclays, Lloyds, National Provincial, and Westminster – were not too far behind.

But around this time, the rationale for the banks' traditional collection of functions disappeared. Securities markets developed. That meant that you did not need to be a big financial services retailer to lend money to large corporations. And the skills involved in the two activities of retail deposit taking and business lending, once rather similar and based on a combination of local presence and knowledge and the stability and security of size and scale, had become quite distinct.

Nobody really noticed. As competitive pressures increased, British banks followed the usual strategies of firms which do not really know what to do. They sought greater size by merger and internal expansion, and engaged in unfocused diversification into new businesses and new areas of the world. All of that was irrelevant, or worse. One final mega-merger created the National Westminster Bank, but the government blocked further concentration. Banks discovered that it is easy to meet targets for growing your balance sheet so long as you are not too bothered about getting your money back. And they lost a packet buying stockbrokers and American banks.

Standard Life, too, had a golden era of success. The business pioneered the retailing of equities to a mass market. That was not what the firm said it was doing; in fact, if it had, it would probably have been stopped. But by packaging equities as a life insurance product, it avoided restrictive regulation and secured effective distribution. It became easier, legally and operationally, to sell shares more directly to individuals. Once that happened, there ceased to be a rationale for linking the three main things Standard Life did: financial services retailing, investment management, and the underwriting of risks.

What National Westminster and Standard Life have in common is that each embraces a range of functions which were sensibly undertaken together at a particular point in history, but for which the rationale of combination has now disappeared. And each business has found that when you unpick the individual things they do, most of them are performed better by someone else.

So what should firms faced with these kinds of strategic dilemmas do? The key requirement is to identify which of the many activities such a firm will be engaged in are ones in which it has an ongoing competitive advantage. What can you do that others cannot readily do as well? One of the four major British banks of the 1980s – Lloyds – undertook this analysis, understood that its strengths were in retail financial services and small business lending, and quit the more glamorous but less profitable activities which required it to compete with every other bank in the world.

But sometimes strategic dilemmas have no solution. This is difficult for executives to accept, but not all questions have answers. Sometimes the proper job of managers is to preside over an orderly transfer of the activities they control to other firms. This does not often happen quickly or without the costs and uncertainties associated with the takeover process. Perhaps it should.

In 2000, National Westminster Bank, which had been struggling for several years, was acquired by the smaller but aggressive Royal Bank of Scotland. When this essay was written in 1997 Standard Life, a Scottish based mutual company, still appeared to occupy a pre-eminent position in the UK savings market. Three years later it fought off a campaign to demutualise the business. The likely flotation value at the time was put at around £12 bn. The business of Standard Life deteriorated rapidly. In 2004, the chief executive was replaced and a decision was taken to float the company in 2006 at a price equivalent to around half that figure.

Let it be

15 OCTOBER 2003

I never got round to applying for the post of chief executive at Barclays, but I'm glad it was John Varley who got the job instead of me.

Sometimes businesses get stranded like grounded hulks. Large, once successful organisations, proudly carry the attributes of their former glory, but no longer fit their environment. It is a tough job being the captain of such a hulk. Perhaps chief executive of Barclays is such a role.

The most common reason for a stranded business is that technology has changed. Railroads were once great organisations but, once the lorry and the car came along, their rationale largely disappeared. Other businesses become stranded because demand changes, or competitive advantage shifts elsewhere. The Woolworth five-and-dime stores and US Steel faded, not because people didn't want to shop or to buy steel, but because they no longer wanted to shop the Woolworth way and because the Japanese and the Koreans became very good at making steel.

The most problematic of stranded businesses are those which grew big, rich, and often complacent behind regulatory protection which they subsequently lost. Fixed-link telephone companies, once impregnable monopolies, are now everywhere in decline. Terrestrial broadcasting networks will have to be quick on their feet to avoid the same fate.

Strategy gurus urge stranded businesses to reinvent themselves. This was the eloquent theme of Ted Levitt's *The Marketing Imagination*: your market is always growing if you define it sufficiently widely. The makers of buggy whips, faced with decline as the motor car took over from the horse drawn carriage, would have prospered if only they had seen themselves as makers of instruments of correction, or transport accessories.

But this misunderstands the true nature of business success, which involves matching internal capabilities to external environment. There is no reason to think those buggy whip makers would have had skills appropriate to marketing to sadists or producing mascots for car windows. The railroad operators who tried their fortunes in trucking or in aviation did not do well. The revamped business is often as embarrassing as the aged pop star's comeback tour. One stranded business which did successfully reinvent itself – IBM – could do so because its real competitive advantage was in sales and service activities, rather than the hardware with which it was identified: its distinctive capabilities could be applied to a different market.

Barclays, like other big banks, came into being when bank branches were a means of gathering small deposits to lend to big businesses. But the growth of securities markets broke the direct link between deposit taking and lending.

Barclays lost the market for savings accounts to building societies a generation ago. Specialist providers did better at making and selling investment products. The company made a brave shot at developing an investment bank, but BZW never made it into the top tier of UK firms, which were themselves swept away in the American takeover of the City of London. Barclays still has a strong position in current accounts, but a declining share of a declining market.

The credit card business is a source of profits for the foreseeable future. But this is the result of Barclays' success in pioneering the product in the UK three decades ago, and the company is today – entirely rationally – allowing entrants to erode its market share with more competitive products. Perhaps the best business in the portfolio is the index fund management business where economies of scale give competitive advantages to strong incumbents.

A bank founded two centuries ago retains substantial assets – a great name and an irreproducible branch network. But most of the branches now seem to have been converted into restaurants. And reputations are not what they were in the modern financial services market. The lure of short term profits too often seems to outweigh the long run benefits of trust relationships with customers.

So good luck, Mr Varley. Your predecessor has left a good impression mainly by not doing much, and you will probably be wise to follow his example. The best course for the master of a grounded hulk is usually to sit tight.

Business heroes

AL DUNLAP (1)

24 JUNE 1998

If you want a friend get a dog

After graduating from West Point military academy, Dunlap
worked for a number of US corporations before becoming a
corporate troubleshooter in the 1980s. A protégé of Sir James
Goldsmith, a colourful British dealmaker, and later of Kerry
Packer, Dunlap was appointed chief executive of Scott Paper in
1994. Fifteen months later, he announced the acquisition of
Scott by Kimberley Clark. The market value of the company
trebled during his career as CEO. His book, *Mean Business*,
published in 1996 'provides invaluable, must-read lessons
for everyone struggling to meet the tough competitive
challenges of today's business world'.

They called him Chainsaw Al, or Rambo in pinstripes. But last week the chainsaw finally severed Al Dunlap from Sunbeam, the company of which he had most recently been chief executive officer.

I never met Mr Dunlap, but had nevertheless almost come to think of him as an old friend. For over a year now, I have quoted liberally from his book *Mean Business* when I wanted to illustrate the extremes of instrumentalism in business behaviour. After one Oxford lecture I heard one departing listener ask another 'Al Dunlap isn't a real person, is he?' I was never sure whether the man whose views I described was a real person, or a figment of the imagination of his ghost writer. And now, I suppose, I will never know.

Dunlap's training was at West Point, 'the best business school in the world'. Still, he came to appreciate other business schools. Especially when a survey of students voted him the most admired chief executive in America. With unusual modesty, he expressed surprise. Dunlap's first job was as executive officer of a nuclear missile establishment. Perhaps that was the only job in which he didn't fire anything.

After working for Sir James Goldsmith and Kerry Packer, he achieved fame by running Scott Paper for two years, drastically pruning its operations and finally selling the company to rival Kimberley Clark. His most recent company was Sunbeam, a manufacturer of small domestic appliances. The stock price jumped by 60% when he was appointed, he tells us in *Mean Business*. And now, it is more or less back where it was when he joined.

Dunlap had no time for sentimental approaches to modern business. 'The most ridiculous term heard in boardrooms today is stakeholders. Stakeholders! Every time I hear that word, I ask: "how much did they pay for their stake?"' A curious, and limited, view of life. Imagine the Al Dunlap manual of parenthood. 'The most ridiculous notion in child rearing today is that parents have obligations to their children. Whenever I hear that, I ask "how much did children pay?"' Or the Al Dunlap guide to social relationships. 'Friendship! Whenever I heard that word, I ask "how much did friends pay for my friendship?"'

In Dunlap's world, the only kind of relationship is one of commercial exchange: the only reason you might be under obligation to someone else is that the person concerned has paid you money. And there is no doubt that this is what he genuinely believes. 'Sometimes, Packer would say to me, "Al, I have had this relationship my whole life! For God's sake, there goes the relationship! What are you doing to me?" "Kerry", I'd say, "I came over here to do a job!"' Relationships are no part of business life. 'If you want a friend, get a dog. I'm taking no chances, I've got two.' And the cover of his book shows him flanked by his dogs, each one no doubt conscious of where supper comes from.

Dunlap is ludicrous and embarrassing for those who argue that business is a serious activity, intellectually challenging, morally defensible, and demanding of public respect. But his self-parody raises fundamental issues about the nature of modern business.

For those who share at least part of Dunlap's philosophy, business is exclusively instrumental. We may warm to his description of a woman's moist-eyed thanks that the rise in the price of Scott Paper stock would enable her to put her children through college. And feel pleased that twenty years after he had left Sterling, the employees he had laid off bought him drinks to express their gratitude. But it is not these implausible encounters which drive Dunlap. 'If you're in business, you're in business for one thing – to make money.'

The argument which Dunlap caricatures is that there is a fundamental dichotomy between the values of business and those of everyday life. But yet, as the Dunlap story demonstrates, it is not clear that the Dunlap view of business is successful even in its own terms.

I am not sure that Bill Gates' recent book is a better read than Al Dunlap's. But the contrast is instructive. It begins with the title:

Dunlap talks of *Mean Business*, Gates of *The Road Ahead*. Dunlap is interested, above all, in money; Gates is interested, above all, in computers. Dunlap thinks of the established businesses he might close down; Gates of the new businesses he might set up. Gates hopes to dominate the world market for software; Dunlap displays no similar ambition or affection for toilet tissue.

And yet it is Gates, not Dunlap, who is the richest man in America. Success in business is rarely achieved by those who are the most naked in their greed. It goes more often to those who are passionate about the activity itself. Greatness in business, as in any other activity, is achieved by those for whom business is an end, not simply a means.

Dunlap's business hero is Sir James Goldsmith. But in the pantheon of great twentieth-century business figures, Goldsmith will barely merit a footnote. The names we will remember are Henry Ford, who made cars available to a mass market, Akio Morita, who brought consumer electronics into every home, and Bill Gates, who put a computer on every desk. All these business leaders made money for themselves and their stockholders, to be sure, but they made money because they first made things. As Al Dunlap goes into lonely retirement, I almost feel sorry for a man whose epitaph is 'if you want a friend, get a dog'. Even in business, you need friends sometimes.

A second instalment of the Al Dunlap saga can be found at p. 152.

Leadership is all

23 APRIL 2002

Can you name the chief executive officer of Siemens or Matsushita? Or the man who is about to succeed Dr Joachim Milberg? The answers are at the end of this article.

But I doubt if any reader of this article would fail to identify the CEO of Vivendi Universal. Jean-Marie Messier, *moi-même, maître du monde*, abbreviated in France to J6M – a nickname M. Messier likes so much that he used it as the title of his autobiography. As a rule, only sports and pop stars have written autobiographies at the age of 44. But M. Messier sees himself in a similar category. For the head of France's biggest water company to use that position to launch himself as an American media mogul is probably the most brazen feat of self-promotion in business history.

But M. Messier is not the only business leader to seek the limelight. Jack Welch's public relations advisers had barely finished dealing with his book tours when they had to cope with the news of his affair. Richard Branson's face is ubiquitous.

This publicity consciousness is new. A television production company recently planned to feature great business figures of the twentieth century. When they sought advice, they arrived with mock-ups of Branson and of Bill Gates. But as I reeled off a list of great business figures of the twentieth century, it became clear that the idea would never make it to the screen. There was no name recognition for Alfred Sloan, who invented the modern corporation. For Thomas Watson Jr, who created the computer business. For Henri Deterding and Marcus Samuel, who built the first global company. For Alfred Mond, who put together a firm synonymous with British manufacturing industry for half a century. The eyes of the television people only lit up when we got to executives who had the same name as their company, like Henry Ford and Simon Marks.

It has always been the case that many successful people suffer from delusions of self importance. Gerald Ratner's taste for publicity was so great that he could not resist telling the world that the products he sold were crap, and so engineered his own downfall. He has, however, subsequently come to terms with ordinary life.

But the public relations industry brings professionalism to the job of getting names into print. And business has become personalised. If you read American business journals, you would suppose that every Microsoft product is the personal invention of Bill Gates, every action at General Electric an expression of the will of Jack Welch.

This personalisation extends to cases taught in US business schools. They routinely begin with a lonely CEO pacing his roomy thirty-eighth floor office as he wrestles with the future of his business. It is not surprising that MBA students who leave these schools aspire to similar roles for themselves.

But the achievements of businesses like GE owe far more to depth of organisation than to heroic individuals. When Welch took over from Reg Jones at General Electric, Jones was the most admired chief executive in the United States. As was his predecessor, Ralph Cordiner. These were remarkable men. But when a company is always run by remarkable men, what is truly remarkable is the company itself.

There are major cultural differences across the major world economies. In Japan and Germany the chief executive is still seen as the servant of the organisation rather than its master. Few top business people in these countries are public figures. The press relations officers of companies are more often concerned to keep their executives' names out of the papers than to put them in.

France is very different. The tradition of the *grand patron* lingers. The very title *président directeur général* implies the focus on a dominant figure. This can allow matters to spiral out of control. As they did a decade ago at Crédit Lyonnais, whose losses make Enron's collapse look small change. J.Y. Haberer, its PDG, did indeed have the power to say yes, as the bank's advertisements emphasised. But French taxpayers, like Vivendi shareholders and employees, must be wishing that someone else had enjoyed the power to say no.

The development of corporate governance in Britain and the United States has helped restrain excessively powerful individuals. Jacques Attali was pushed out of the European Bank of Research and Development by the English speaking members of the Board. It is less likely today that Ross Johnson of RJR Nabisco would find golf partners by putting America's leading sportsmen on the corporate payroll, or send a corporate jet for his dog. Branson had to take Virgin private, and Stelios Haji-Iaonnou has just discovered that his new institutional shareholders at EasyJet will not tolerate his public style.

And this is how it should be. Jim Collins' recent study of corporate transformations picked out humility as a characteristic of his most successful leaders – people who built up businesses rather than themselves. Collins' hero is Darwin Smith, the uncharismatic CEO who made Kimberley Clark an effective competitor to Procter and Gamble. And Heinrich Pierer of Siemens, and Kunio Nakamura of Matsushita run pretty good businesses. We should wish good fortune and continued low profile to Helmut Panke when he takes over the top spot at BMW next month.

Messier was fired from his position at Vivendi in July 2002, with a severance package estimated at $20 million. He later agreed to return the money as part of a settlement of a civil fraud suit brought by the SEC. The entertainment activities of Vivendi were subsequently dismantled. General Electric bought several of its subsidiaries. Dr Panke's name was misspelled in the originally printed version of this article. No one ever pointed out the error. At the time of writing Dr Panke continues the distinguished career at BMW which he began in 1982.

Business heroes

CARLY FIORINA

15 FEBRUARY 2005

Carly Fiorina (1954 –) graduated from Stanford and joined AT&T in 1980 after completing her MBA at the University of Maryland. She went to Lucent Technologies after the business was spun off from AT&T and was headhunted as CEO and President of Hewlett Packard. After the unsuccessful merger with Compaq, Fiorina became an increasingly controversial figure. Her contract was terminated by the Hewlett Packard board in 2005.

The share price of Hewlett Packard jumped when Carly Fiorina was appointed in 1999 and it jumped again when she was fired last week. In the meantime, it has fallen by more than half. Ms Fiorina was headhunted by Hewlett Packard in 1999 from Lucent, then flying high. HP, once the most revered name in Silicon Valley, was looking for an exceptional person to restore the company's fortunes.

Beauty contests for executive talent are common today. The competitive hunt for the best people in other companies supposes that general management skills are more important than specific organisational knowledge, and that supremely talented individuals can single-handedly transform businesses with their vision and charisma. Rakesh Khurana's *Searching for a Corporate Saviour*, and Henry Mintzberg's *Managers not MBAs*, cruelly dissect these fallacies.

Ms Fiorina did the things expected of transformational leaders. She embarked on a public relations offensive. Within the company, 'coffee with Carly' took over from 'the HP way'. On public appearances, the immaculately tousled hair of America's leading female executive quickly made her the most readily recognised business figure in the country.

She demanded rounds of cost reduction from subordinates. Sometimes such economies lead to greater efficiency, sometimes they undermine the long-term prospects of the business. In the absence of intimate knowledge of the organisation in question, it is hard to tell. No matter: in either case the process enhances earnings per share in the short run.

But the real test of the corporate saviour is whether she can land the big deal. Ms Fiorina first made a pitch for the consulting business of PwC, only to learn that many of the opinionated folk in that business were unenthusiastic about a merger with a manufacturing company under her leadership. But she completed the acquisition of the ailing Compaq. The results were disappointing and last week Ms Fiorina paid the price. The lesson from Hewlett Packard is not simply that Ms Fiorina was not up to the job. It is that the role in which she so willingly cast herself is not one in which anyone is likely to succeed.

It is not always a mistake to hire an outsider for the top job. This move can be effective when the culture of an organisation has become so dysfunctional that it is necessary to start again. But the outsider who brings his or her own blueprint will almost invariably fail: the better approach to this task is to find and release the frustrated energy already present in the business. As the American pro-consuls in Iraq can testify, such reconstruction is no easy task. There is also a business role for larger-than-life personalities – like Bill Hewlett or Dave Packard. Such figures make their principal contribution in the early stages of corporate development, when the positioning, identity and values of the business need to be established.

But there is a world of difference between the attributes appropriate to the founding entrepreneur and the political skills demanded of the effective manager of a larger organisation. Henry Ford defined the products and technology of the automobile business but Alfred Sloan at General Motors defined the structures needed to run it, something of which Ford himself was quite incapable. It has been fashionable – and lucrative – for consultants, gurus and especially chief executives to blur this distinction between entrepreneur and the professional manager. But the results of that elision have generally – as at HP – been unsuccessful and frequently – as at WorldCom or Vivendi – disastrous.

Great businesses depend on the talents of thousands of people, not just one. Their management requires a multiplicity of incompatible talents: both vision and attention to detail, both emotional intelligence and analytic capability, both self-confidence and self criticism. The most effective managers possess an idiosyncratic balance of attributes appropriate for the situations they face, and the range of abilities successful corporations require must be sought across a team rather than in a single personality. Rows of suits (male or female) are less photogenic than Carly Fiorina but they are what really makes modern business work.

The capabilities of the firm

Corporate success is the product of the match between the distinctive capabilities of the firm and its external environment. This section of the book is concerned with the ways in which businesses can develop and exploit distinctive capabilities: through strategic assets – scarce factors or resources or favourable market structures: through brands and reputations: and through their architecture, the structure of relationships which they establish with their customers, suppliers or employees.

The bubbles in Champagne

4 APRIL 1997

When Stanley Matthews retired from football, there was still an agreement between clubs to limit the earnings of players to not much more than the national average weekly wage of all workers. Today, successful sportsmen are fabulously wealthy. Football clubs are investments. Bernie Ecclestone, a racing promoter, has plans to float the business which organises Formula 1 motor racing for a reported £2.5bn. What is going on?

Returns go where there is scarcity. You can match all but the finest champagnes with cheaper sparkling wines from other parts of France or the New World. But the sales efforts of the great champagne houses of Rheims and Epernay established *grandes marques* – like Moët et Chandon and Veuve Cliquot – and made champagne, even today, a drink for a special occasion.

But to whom did the profits these activities created belong? At first, they accrued to the firms which had created these legendary brands. But although the firms controlled the names of their houses, they did not control the name of champagne. That belonged to a province of France. The system of *appellation controlée* ensured that only wine from that region could carry the name champagne. There is only a limited amount of wine-growing land in the Champagne region. The returns bubbled back to the scarce factor, and the value of Champagne vineyards now far exceeds that of land of equivalent quality on the wrong side of the departmental border.

In the 1980s, the growers tried to grab a larger share of the champagne spoils. By selling directly to shops and customers, they could bypass one element in the chain that was no longer scarce –

the distribution capability of the great champagne houses. They could not get all the profits, because they did not have access to the great names. But very palatable champagne labelled with obscure brands appeared in supermarkets, and not everyone felt ashamed to celebrate with a sparkling bottle from Sainsbury or Tesco.

For a time, growers and champagne houses together tried to earn higher returns than the market would support. The premium sought for champagne became excessive and choked off demand, or left it in the bottle. Eventually pricing became more realistic and the various parties agreed on a distribution of the premium between the *vignobles* of the Champagne region and the mystique of the *grandes marques*.

The spread of video recorders in the same period massively increased revenues from the sale of films. Who benefited from these increased revenues? Not, as people were first inclined to think, video distributors and video stores. Look at the lists of bankrupt companies of the last few years and you will find many failed ventures of video entrepreneurs. You need to look for the scarce factors, and these are not found in street corner distribution: there is no scarcity of premises from which to distribute bad movies. The scarce factors were the names and the talent needed to create blockbusters. The cost of making films rose in line with the rise in film revenues. The new money went to pay Arnold Schwarzenegger and indulge Stephen Spielberg.

Some factors, like the land in Champagne or the genius of a Spielberg, are intrinsically scarce. Some are made scarce, others cease to be scarce. The history of broadcasting illustrates all these things. For almost all the twentieth century, broadcasting was dominated by shortage of spectrum on the airwaves. Governments allocated that scarce factor. Initially they allocated it to themselves, or their agencies, and most early transmissions came from public sector broadcasters. Later they began to allocate it to private companies. Lord Thomson, one of the early franchisees of commercial television in the UK, famously described what he had been given as 'a licence to print money'. More recently, scarcity of spectrum lost importance as there came to be many new ways of sending electronic messages.

So who benefited? Again, the rule is to look for scarcity. You saw the rising price of scarcity when the cast of *Gardeners' Question Time* migrated to Classic FM. And you see it again when the price paid for the TV rights to famous movies, or league sports, is bid up. But do not buy football teams indiscriminately. That is the equivalent of setting up a video store to benefit from the video boom, and is already burning fingers in just the same way. Search for the scarce factors; and you find them in the great clubs, like Manchester United, and the great players. The returns from the massive increase in revenues associated with football will end up there. The larger market widens the differentials between the best and the average.

So is Formula 1 motor racing worth its reported flotation tag? Bernie Ecclestone is no doubt right when he reckons that competition in the sporting rights market will lead to a similar increase in what is spent on motor sport. But ask again where the scarce factors are. There are some drivers, like Michael Schumacher, with truly exceptional talents. There are some circuits – not many – whose glamour cannot be reproduced by either Melbourne or Adelaide – Monaco, perhaps Spa and Monza. Formula 1 needs them more than they need Formula 1.

And scarcest of all are the great teams. You cannot have a Grand Prix without Ferrari, Williams, McLaren and Benetton. Shell was willing to pay Schumacher's £16 million salary to put its logo on the side of his Ferrari. At the moment these teams are battling over shares of the television spoils and eventually they will win. And is Bernie Ecclestone scarce? Or is he just motor racing's equivalent of the champagne house, without the same cachet attaching to his name?

The attempt to float Formula 1 was abandoned. The financial arrangements surrounding Ecclestone's business have been the subject of controversy and dispute ever since.

Fine distinctions

4 OCTOBER 2000

Every day, photographs from the Sydney Olympic Games show joy on the faces of the winners and the anguish of the losers. Yet it is a sporting cliché that the margin between victory and defeat is small. In a typical event, someone whose speed is 99% of the gold medallist's will go home empty-handed. Someone who runs 95% as fast as the winner will be an average club athlete and will not be in Australia at all.

For many purposes, differences of this magnitude do not matter. The runners in the Greek Olympics spent the time between games delivering letters. If Achilles could run with the speed of a hundred arrows, while Herodotus could only rate ninety-five, their respective employers would barely notice. Possibly Achilles delivered a few more letters, and earned a little more. But less than five per cent more letters, and for less than five per cent more pay.

A race is an artificial environment in which small differences in talent are greatly magnified. Only when we put Achilles and Herodotus side by side and give them exactly the same task can we see the difference between them. And then – because it is the winning, not the taking part that *really* matters – the rewards of Achilles are a large multiple of those of Herodotus.

This contrast between the race and the mail has its analogy in business. In some activities, output is more or less proportional to input. In others, a slight superiority of input is translated into an enormous difference in the perceived value of the output. These latter activities are typically the ones that yield big profits for successful companies and high earnings for able individuals.

Pharmaceutical supply is, and almost always has been, an

exceptionally profitable market. Not for all companies, however. The history of the industry is littered with failed entrants. The profits of pharmaceutical companies have been derived mainly by a few businesses from a small number of blockbuster drugs. When you are ill, you want the gold medallist, not the bronze or the also ran.

The car market is different. There is no agreement on which is the best car. Some people want performance, some comfort, others go mainly on appearance. And even if we all thought a Rolls-Royce or Ferrari was best, most of us cannot afford one. Lada and Skoda sold cars everyone agreed were inferior; they just had to accept lower prices. The Ladas of the pharmaceutical business never even get to market.

The runners-up set the baseline by which the winner is judged. We need Herodotus at the Olympics because there must be someone for Achilles to beat. We also need Herodotus in the post office because Achilles can't deliver all the mail himself. To ensure a constant supply of new drugs, there must be hundreds of failures as well as the few successes. But the difference between the successful and the baseline is much larger in pharmaceuticals, as at the Olympics, than in mail delivery. And that means the overall level of earnings is higher too. So it is not just that the best pharmaceutical companies earn high returns. The overall level of industry profits is high.

These differences in the economic characteristics of processes also have an important influence on the distribution of earnings. In the courtroom there is a winner and a loser. A small difference in the talents of your attorney can become a crucial difference in the result. That is why the best lawyers are well paid. I can complete a golf round with only 25% more shots than Tiger Woods, but the gap between our earnings on the professional circuit is a lot wider than 25%. And J.K. Rowling's royalties are orders of magnitude larger than those of other children's novelists. Law, golf and popular novels are activities in which small variations in talent lead to large differences in return.

But while I want my company's audit done well, I am not sure about paying a large premium for it. The green keeper who mows Tiger Woods' course 25% faster gets paid only 25% more. And the bookshop that sells twice as many copies of Ms Rowling's latest work does twice, but only twice, as well.

So how can we distinguish the Olympic athlete from the fleet-of-foot mailman? There are two elements that distinguish the race from the mail. One is agreement on the characteristics that distinguish the best from the less good. This is more true of drugs than of automobiles, of spreadsheets than of search engines.*

The other is that a small difference in quality translates into a large difference in the perceived value of the product. This happens mostly when the product cost is small relative to the implications of the outcome. It is well worth paying more for a drug that will keep you alive, or for a lawyer who will keep you out of jail. Similarly, a financial adviser who will make you rich should command a large premium to his more pedestrian rivals. And it is enough that you believe they might secure you continued health, or freedom, or wealth. It doesn't have to be true. Above all, avoid situations where quantity can be substituted for quality. That's why the guy who mows the green for Tiger Woods doesn't earn as much as Tiger even though he is just as essential to the Masters' championship.

---

* This did seem to be true in 1997: it is not true in 2006, when Google dominates. But I suspect the future may yet lie with more differentiated search engines.

A rose by any other name

6 DECEMBER 1996

What is a brand? A rose by any other name, Shakespeare pointed out, would smell as sweet. There is a difference between a name and a brand. You are reading an article by John Kay. But John Kay makes the transition from name on the masthead to brand only when attaching it to the contents persuades you to read the article, or pay attention to it – while you would ignore the same piece if it appeared under someone else's name. Once that happens – but only when it happens – I have a brand with a value.

You will not admire the scent of a stinging nettle because I label it a rose, and that is why rose is a description of a fine product, rather than a brand. You use electricity because it illuminates your light bulb, not because it is called electricity: you go to Euston Station because that is where the trains for Birmingham and Manchester are, not because it is Euston Station. Roses, electricity and Euston Station all have values, but not brand values.

A brand is worth more than a functionally equivalent product. You pay far more for a bottle of Chanel No 5 than for a bottle of liquid whose smell is indistinguishable. And that is what makes clear to us that roses, electricity and Euston are not brands. No sensible person would shell out cash to be allowed to describe a nettle as a rose, to label coal as solid electricity, or to call a bus depot Euston Station. But you would like to be able to call your fizzy soft drink Coca-Cola, to offer legal advice under the brand name of Linklater and Paines, and to put up a Hertz sign outside your car hire agency. People can and do pay money for access to these brands. The brand adds value even if the product is unchanged.

So what gives a brand that value? Why would people pay more when they can get the same for less? Most often, marketeers will tell us, because they do not think it is the same. You feel seductive when you splash on Chanel No 5, but you will never derive the same confidence from a whiff of anonymous scent, even if you would need a trained perfumier to tell the difference.

Perhaps. Perfume is certainly a commodity that appeals to irrational instincts. And there are goods where the brand encourages people to make statements about themselves to others. I am irresistible, I say, as I put on my designer fragrance. I am a merchant banker, I say, as I climb out of my BMW. I am a juvenile lout, I say, as I down a glass of extra strong lager. I am handsome, I say, as I don my Levi jeans.

Some brands are of this kind. Mostly, these brands apply to commodities like clothes, drinks, cars and cigarettes which you consume consciously in the presence of other people. And as with any signal, the brand as signal has its value eroded when people use the signal in misleading ways. Since the shop will sell you Levis whether you are handsome or not, the illusion that you will be handsome if you wear them is hard to sustain. To survive, the brand as signal has to remain exclusive. Either because not everyone wishes to give the signal – football fans drink extra-strength lagers, the Queen Mother does not – or because the signal keeps people out by of its expense. The most enduring of such brands are symbols of affluence – Rolls-Royce, Moët et Chandon, Hermes.

But while you certainly need to be affluent to enjoy the services of a city law firm, not many people use Linklater and Paines in the hope that their friends will be impressed to see them coming out of their offices. Or hire a Hertz car in order to display the discreet No 1 logo in the rear windows of their Fiat Panda. You go to Linklaters because you think you will get good advice. You hire from Hertz because you don't expect that their car will break down and you know that they will fix it if it does.

The most important function of brands is quality certification. Other lawyers may give you equally good advice, but you can't be sure. Other firms may rent reliable cars, but when you visit a foreign city for the first time, how do you know? For goods where it is difficult for consumers to judge quality for themselves, the reputation associated with a powerful brand may have considerable value. Most of the brands that command large price premia are of this kind. They are found in industries where product quality is important to consumers but is not easy to assess, as for legal services, medicines, or financial services. Or where people care about the quality of the goods concerned but don't like discussing that with their friends, as for toilet paper, contraceptives and sanitary towels.

And that is the mechanism by which names turn into brands. No doubt Mr Linklater and Mr Paine were fine lawyers in their time. Other good lawyers realised that they could make the level of their skills known to potential clients by attaching themselves to the coat tails of Mr Linklater and Mr Paine. And Mr Linklater and Mr Paine themselves could make a turn by selling out the services of such lawyers for more than they had to pay them. This process enabled the reputation of Mr Linklater and Mr Paine to outlive the individuals concerned.

A solicitor can turn with confidence to Halsbury's *Laws of England*, not so much because he trusts the integrity and reliability of Lord Halsbury – who has been dead for the best part of a century – but because the publishers have an incentive to maintain the value of the brand Lord Halsbury established. As the *Financial Times* has an incentive to maintain the quality and reliability of the material which appears on its pages. And John Kay has an incentive to keep up the standard of his columns. That way, he might turn a name into a brand.

Italy off the beaten track

FROM *Foundations of Corporate Success*

The Lumezzane valley in Brescia in northern Italy is not on many tourist itineraries. Although its natural scenery is attractive, its calm is shattered by the noise from hundreds of small metal-working establishments, which often continues late into the night. In parts of the valley it seems as though almost every house has a small factory attached. Casual tourists would probably be surprised that this style of economic organisation had lasted so long. They might plan to revisit Lumezzane in a few years' time when these industries had finally been swept away by the forces of international competition, reinforced by global marketing and the research and development and quality control resources which only large firms can command.

That judgment could hardly be more wrong. Far from threatening Lumezzane, the opening of international markets has brought unparalleled prosperity. Most of the output of the valley is exported and the region is one of the richest in Italy. Nor does it rely simply on traditional craft skills. Lumezzane is a market leader in a range of sophisticated metal-manufacturing products including valves, taps, and the customised machine tools used in their production. The structure of relationships between the small firms of the Lumezzane valley, often specialised in a single component of the final product, which gives each access to the knowledge, abilities, and resources of the whole, has given Lumezzane a continuing competitive advantage in its markets.

That competitive advantage derives from the flexibility and speed of response available through relational contracts – business agreements which are enforced, not by the law, but by the needs of the parties to go on doing business with each other. Relational contracts require continuity and stability of relationships: continuity and stability which are well-known features of Japanese business, and firms such as Toyota and NEC are surrounded by their keiretsu, or supplier group.

Just in time inventory management, as developed by Toyota, is a striking example of a structure possible only under relational contracting. Urgent demand requires the urgent willing response of the partner in a long-term relationship, not the hard-nosed spot contract which can be achieved when the opposing party is most vulnerable. In the United States, customised components are generally manufactured in-house or by wholly owned subsidiaries of the assembler (Monteverde and Teece, 1982). In Japan these items are produced by independent members of the keiretsu, who are willing to take the risk of establishing dedicated production facilities and installing transaction-specific assets. The same supply processes are achieved through classical contracting in one country, through relational contracting in the other.

Japan has a long tradition of co-operative groupings of companies, originating in the zaibatsu which were dissolved by the Allies after the Second World War. Although there is some presumption in favour of inter-group trading among these networks, members of them also trade extensively with Japanese companies outside the group. The power of the network seems to rest partly in the exchange of information through it (hence the emphasis on 'one-set-ism', the requirement that the group contains precisely one company in each sector), and on the ready ability of the group to support transactions which benefit from relational contracting, such as financing, overseas distribution and joint ventures.

The Japanese experience, and the contrast between Japan and the United States, illustrates the degree to which relational contracting is part of the broader commercial and social environment. Geographical proximity is important to networking, although the role it plays is not entirely obvious. Since transporting ties is neither slow nor expensive, why are most Italian ties produced in a single small region? At first sight it seems absurd that at a time when capital markets have become international and worldwide communication of data, funds, and information has become instantaneous, the financial institutions of the world should be concentrated in tiny and fabulously expensive areas of lower Manhattan and eastern London.

What lies behind this is the need to establish trust and penalise opportunism in a network of relational contracts, which is facilitated if business relationships are supported by a corresponding network of social relationships. We are all more inclined to trust people we know; a view which is partly based on instinct and emotion, partly on our capacity to make our own judgments (we are also inclined to mistrust some people we know), and partly on a rational calculation that people are less likely to cheat us if by doing so they sacrifice a social reputation as well as a commercial one.

The City of London's pre-eminence rested on the homogeneity of background and values created by the English class system and the English school system. These factors may also explain why conscious attempts to emulate the competitive advantages of networking through replication are rarely successful. The extensive entertainment which is integral to Japanese business similarly serves to reinforce relational contracts.

These structures of relational contracts, the architecture of the firm, are a common distinctive capability and, when matched to appropriate markets, a source of competitive advantage. Some social environments are more conducive to the development of competitive advantage through architecture than others. Since the essence of architecture is that organisations or groups of organisations have values – social and economic – distinct from those of their members, there is a direct conflict between individualism and the creation of architecture. This conflict is reinforced by the absence of powerful sanctions against opportunistic behaviour in an individualistic environment.

Competitive strengths based on these architectures are therefore relatively rare in those environments where the prevailing ethos is strongly individualistic. Where they exist – as in the financial sector, in networking activities in less developed countries, and in the performance of companies with a very distinctive corporate ethos – the activities concerned are commonly viewed by outsiders with a degree of hostility and suspicion. Nepotism is a term of abuse, contact networks are corrupt, and the organisation man is regarded with uneasy laughter. While US firms most often seek competitive advantage from innovation, and derive it through brands and reputation, the competitive advantages of European and Japanese businesses are more often secured through their architecture.

Brakes and signals

12 MAY 1999

Before Bill Gates, there was ... George Westinghouse. Westinghouse was as much a titan of American industry in the latter part of the nineteenth century as Gates is now. Like Microsoft, Westinghouse controlled one central component of the new infrastructure. Most railroad cars and trucks used Westinghouse brakes, as most personal computers use Microsoft's operating system. Both Gates and Westinghouse made a fortune from the market position they established.

Safe operation of a train requires that all coupled carriages or trucks can be stopped by a single system controlled from the locomotive. Westinghouse's compressed air braking system was one such mechanism. But to use rolling stock efficiently, each company should fit the same system to all its vehicles.

If rolling stock was to move freely between networks, all companies needed to adhere to the same standard. Compatibility was particularly important for freight, where you hoped to be able to ship a truck from one side of the United States to the other without unloading and reloading it along the way.

The position of the Burlington railroad, which operated lines out of Chicago, was critical. The opening of the prairies had been one of the great achievements of the railway age. The company's network was also the gateway between the eastern and western states. Once Westinghouse had persuaded Burlington to adopt his system, Westinghouse air brakes were adopted almost universally. Vacuum brakes – which some thought superior – lost the standards war.

IBM was to Bill Gates what Burlington was to Westinghouse. IBM's sponsorship of MS-DOS promoted that operating system as effectively in the personal computer world as Burlington's adoption of the Westinghouse system did in the American railroad industry. The copyrights that protect Microsoft's source code correspond to the coupling patents that enabled Westinghouse to defend his system. Vacuum braking was the nineteenth-century analogy of the Apple Mac. Its followers were devotees, but they became a shrinking minority.

The successes of Westinghouse and Microsoft are unusual events in business history. Both markets were bound to produce a dominant standard because of the need for compatibility. All American railroads wanted the most widely adopted braking system. All personal computer users want the operating system with the most software. The winners happened to be Westinghouse's brakes and Microsoft's MS-DOS and Windows. There was nothing inevitable about the victory of these companies, but if central braking systems and personal computing were to take off someone would inevitably achieve market dominance.

Many markets have compatibility standards. Some are common property – the 4´8½˝ railroad gauge was an even more important compatibility standard than the common braking system, but the spacing of the rails was not something anyone could 'own'. Some standards are determined by government regulation – such as the size and number of lines on a television picture. Most proprietary standards are freely licensed, and successful only because they are. VHS beat Sony's Betamax video recorder, and Visa credit cards are more widely used than Amex, because JVC (owner of VHS) and Visa encouraged other users whereas Sony (owner of Betamax) and American Express sought to maintain control of the standard for themselves.

The nearly unique achievement of first George Westinghouse and then Bill Gates was to establish a universal standard while maintaining tight proprietary control. For each, the result was not only a huge personal fortune, but a platform for expansion into other markets. But that expansion carried risks and dangers.

Westinghouse hoped to replicate his success with brakes by achieving dominance in the supply of signalling equipment to US railroads. He failed. Signals are fundamentally different from brakes. There are standards in signals, of course – it really does matter that everyone knows that red means stop and green means go and that there aren't places where it is the other way round. But no-one owns, or can own, that element of the standard.

There is no need for a common standard in signal operation. You could use different designs of signal along the same line, and railroads did. They were free to pick the best signal. Or what their engineers, an idiosyncratic lot, thought was the best signal. With brakes, you were forced to choose the one everyone else had chosen.

And that poses an issue for Bill Gates, or anyone else planning to invest in the next generation of information technology. Are you selling a brake, or a signal? For brakes compatibility is more important than excellence, and market dominance is inevitable – not necessarily for the best product, but for the product that is adopted by IBM or the Burlington railroad. For signals your own assessment of product quality guides your decision, and it matters little whether or not others have made the same decision. In a market for brakes, any common standards will be firmly entrenched. In a market for signals, a better product can quickly displace an established one.

There are a few brakes in the new world. But more signals. Be sure to know which you are dealing with. George Westinghouse ultimately overstretched himself and lost control of his empire.

British Telecom

29 MAY 2003

So BT is to return to its roots – as Britain's fixed link telephone company. It has been an exciting journey for the company's shareholders, and like all the best adventures, it finishes back where it began – operationally and financially. The two million small savers who took their money from the building society to subscribe to the first major utility privatisation are today more or less where they would have been if they had simply left it there.

Soon after that 1984 flotation British Telecom decided to become a vertically integrated telecoms company, providing not only the calls but the hardware that made it possible. It bought a cluster of equipment makers. But there was nothing much in common between a utility with its origins as government depart-ment and a competitive manufacturing business. In 1991 BT acquired a new strategic direction, complete with Pied Piper logo. The hardware businesses were sold.

The new vision was of a global horizontally diversified telecoms service provider. BT – British Telecom was now much too parochial a name – would provide your voice and data require-ments, whatever they were, anywhere in the world. The company took a large stake in McCaw, then the largest American mobile phone operator, and other telecom services companies. These acquisitions did not work out either. There was no reason why anyone should want to buy their mobile phone in Chicago from the organisation that provided domestic connections in Cardiff. In 1994, McCaw was bought by an American telephone company.

Globalisation, outsourcing and alliances were now on the lips of every business person. BT's next new strategy combined all three.

The thesis was that multinational companies were restructuring their activities on functional, not territorial, lines. They would want to outsource the whole of their data and telecoms requirements. Only a company with partners around the world could meet these needs. The future lay in a network of alliances, such as that found in airlines or accountancy.

There is no evidence that there was or will ever be a large demand for this capability. Large companies were mostly relieved to be free of their local telecoms monopoly, and preferred to employ their own professional buyers to choose the best services and deals. Concert, the flagship of BT's alliances, was expensively wound up last year.

In 1997, the strategy changed again. MCI, BT's erstwhile partner, was snatched from the company's grasp by the soon-to-be notorious Bernie Ebbers. This transaction was then described as the world's largest takeover bid, although the mountains of WorldCom paper Ebbers used to pay for it subsequently proved worthless. BT's new vision was of a rapidly consolidating world telecoms industry. There would be a race to be the successful consolidator and BT's ambition was to lead the race. An acquisitions spree followed in which telecoms companies bought each other at ever more ridiculous prices. In 2000 the bubble burst and most of the new telecoms conglomerates, including BT itself, were broken up to placate their bankers.

None of BT's four consecutive phases of strategy was successful. Worse, none really deserves to be taken seriously. BT never encountered a management fad it did not like. The company fell victim to the consultant and business school rhetoric so effectively satirised by Lucy Kellaway. Neither intellectually rigorous nor rooted in the real world, this language delivers exhortations which combine superficiality and urgency: established knowledge is obsolete, act now before it is Too Late. Its texts have titles like 'Leading the Revolution' and 'Only the Paranoid Survive', its practitioners dispense clichés polished to vacuity by endless repetition.

There is something to be said for encapsulating a company's strategy in a pithy slogan. But in BT, as for many businesses of its time, the slogan was the strategy. The practical consequence was that the company used the strong credit rating attributable to its domestic fixed link monopoly to make strings of fruitless acquisitions until the credit rating became too weak to support any more.

Well remunerated executives, consultants and bankers sat round mahogany tables late into the night, fired by the excitement of the latest value-destroying deal. But beneath this frothy irrelevance others were grappling with running the business. BT's core activities are incomparably better managed than at privatisation, more efficient, more customer friendly. If BT's new strategy means a period free from grand visions in which operational managers are left to get on with their job, its future is brighter than for many years.

The market environment

Corporate success is the product of the match between the distinctive capabilities of the firm and its external environment. This sector of the book is concerned with the external environment. The 'five forces' approach of Michael Porter, which emphasises entrants, suppliers, buyers, substitutes as external influences on rivalry between competitors, is one way to assess the market and the industry. The approach illustrated here is rather different. The fundamental question is 'where are the scarce factors in this industry?' The answer, which varies considerably across different activities, directs us to the sources of competitive advantage. The essays here pose that question for diverse industries – pharmaceuticals, media, retailing and business services.

Pharmaceuticals

23 NOVEMBER 2004

When the FT listed the fifty largest businesses by market capitalisation in May 2004, eight pharmaceutical companies were included When it listed the fifty most respected businesses last week, only one of these eight – Johnson and Johnson – made it into the list.

For an industry that depends more than most on public trust, that reveals a problem. The problem was vividly illustrated on the front page of the *Financial Times* on that very day, where Ray Gilmartin of Merck was defending his company's handling of Vioxx, its now withdrawn painkiller. A decade ago, Merck was always among the most admired companies. It is no longer in the FT's most respected fifty, and is struggling to keep its place in the top fifty by market capitalisation.

Not only has the pharmaceutical industry lost status with other business leaders: it is under wide-ranging attack. In books from novelist John le Carré, journalist Merrill Goozner, and doctor Marcia Angell. In the public stance of prosecutor Eliot Spitzer and film-maker Michael Moore, as well as by Food and Drug Administration officials critical of the integrity of its research, anti-globalisation protesters critical of its ethics, and senior citizens critical of its prices.

George Merck, Mr Gilmartin's predecessor, understood the implicit deal between the industry and the public when he said 'we try never to forget that medicine is for the people. It is not for the profits. The profits follow, and if we have remembered that, they have never failed to appear.' And for decades the formula worked well: the industry produced a stream of new drugs and received a stream of dollars in return.

But these sentiments were out of fashion in the 1990s. Financial markets required corporate activity, aka mergers and acquisitions, and double digit growth in earnings per share. So the companies spent the money the public had given them for research on buying each other. They raised the market prices of successful drugs. They hired representatives in short skirts to promote their products. They focused on imitative versions of established therapies at the expense of genuine innovation.

Keeping treatment out of the reach of terminally ill patients in southern Africa is bad public relations. Companies that derive their revenues from governments and the sick must take special care with their pricing strategies. Selective dissemination of research results undermines trust. It is surprising that generous remuneration for senior executives in the pharmaceutical industry failed to attract people with the acumen to see these consequences. Or perhaps, motivated by share options, they did not care.

The pharmaceutical industry, more than most, does rely on exceptional talent: but these gifted people are in laboratories, not boardrooms. And while they were once content to work in large drug companies for modest salaries, they are now able to attract venture capital for their own show.

Tougher regulation might restore confidence in the industry but the companies have sought to undermine regulation by political action. Drug company lobbyists have won some victories. But members of Congress ultimately need the votes of senior citizens even more than they need campaign finance. Healthcare reform is not an issue which will go away.

The funding and technology of health is now likely to develop in ways that marginalize the giants. Today one dollar is retained in profit and one spent on marketing for every dollar that goes to research. You need to be very confident of the quality of the research dollar for that equation to represent value for money. And confidence in the productivity of the research of large pharmaceutical companies has declined.

The old model worked best for traditional blockbusters, products that relieved but did not cure the chronic illnesses of the affluent, like hypertension, depression and flagging virility. Future drugs will be targeted more at individuals and at rarer conditions, cocktails of treatments will take the place of single therapies. Perhaps, also, the West will recognise that simple drugs for debilitating illnesses are among the most effective forms of foreign aid. All these developments suit the public and philanthropic funding of basic research, with incremental innovation and peer review, better than the proprietary programmes directed towards mass market drugs for which big pharmaceutical companies with strategies increasingly similar to those of other consumer goods businesses have been well suited. The fat market capitalisations of these corporations reflect their past achievements and present profits, but not their future prospects.

Television reality

19 NOVEMBER 2003

Our screens are filled with unreal reality shows, talent spotting contests in which a microscope is required to spot any talent at all, and quiz shows which vie to see how rude a presenter can be to the contestants. It was encouraging to hear that one of the participants in the new Channel Four series, *Boss Swap*, had walked out prematurely. Perhaps there are, after all, some limits to the humiliation people will endure for the chance to appear on television.

We are seeing the death throes of the television channel. For most of the twentieth century it was difficult and expensive to deliver electronic signals to consumers. You could reach them only by filling the air with broadcast signals. But transmission was costly and broadcast spectrum limited. That is why we all had to see the same material at the same time.

But traditional television channels are no longer special. Many more broadcast programmes, terrestrial and satellite, can be accommodated, and the costs of accessing them has fallen. You can bring a video cassette or DVD into your house. More and more electronic media can be accessed through telephone lines and cable. The day is not far off when it will be cheaper to deliver electronic material than to distribute books, music or films. For spammers, file sharers and bloggers, it has already arrived.

So television networks – the people who choose what we all see – are losing the power they once enjoyed. The manager of the channel will give way to the publisher, the electronic equivalents of the people who search out new authors, promote composers and bands, or finance and publicise films. These other media industries – books, music, cinema – share common characteristics.

Most novelties fail, but some remain in demand for several years and a few become perennial favourites – the classic novels, compositions and movies which constitute the enduring repertoire of our culture.

The networks which promoted channels were vertically integrated businesses – they conceived, made, marketed and broadcast the programmes, and controlled costs and revenues from the beginning of the value chain to the end. The functions of publishers are more limited. There is no more reason why publishing companies should be involved in the delivery of product than there is for music companies to be hi-fi manufacturers, for studios to own cinemas, or for writers to operate bookshops. Occasionally some investment bank will spot a deal or strategy planner think vertical integration is a good idea – hence Sony Music and Barnes and Noble classics. But the skills of audio manufacture are very different from those of promoting rap bands, and running a chain of book stores demands talents different from those needed to write *Wuthering Heights*.

That is not how most established broadcasters see it. Like most companies, they want to adapt the market to the structure of their organisation, rather than the other way round. So they are wedded to vertical integration and to continuing their role as broadcasters.

Broadcasting – the transmission of the same material simultaneously to a very large audience – is still a cost effective mechanism for distributing the Cup Final, a Royal Wedding, a Presidential address to the nation, or the aftermath of September 11 2001. Everyone's needs are much the same, and these are shared experiences, where we enjoy or commiserate together. But there are not many events like these.

So broadcasters have responded by creating television programmes designed as news in themselves. The latest developments in a soap opera, sex in the Big Brother house, cheating on quiz programmes, are not news of an elevated kind. But they are reported in the tabloid press and you need to see these programmes to participate in workplace gossip or bar room conversation.

There will always be a few lonely people who send wreaths on the death of a soap opera character. But vicarious reality is a second rate experience, and the formulaic nature of these programmes leads increasing numbers of people to reach for the channel change button. To sustain interest, the formats must become more exotic, the events ever more bizarre. These programmes are a last ditch attempt to keep a dying format – the television channel – alive. Wouldn't it be better – for both the organisations and the viewers – if quality networks embraced a future as publishers of quality rather than broadcasters of rubbish?

Best sellers

Thomas Edison, founder of General Electric, invented a process by which you could record sounds and voices and play them over and over again. The electrical media business was born. And now, after dabbling successfully in aero engines, medical equipment and financial services, General Electric will return to these roots. Through Universal Studios, Jeff Immelt and his colleagues are now promoters of Eminem and producers of Seabiscuit.

The prospect that media industries would inevitably be dominated by large international conglomerates has for long excited investment bankers and depressed creative people. But, more recently, it has seemed to be yesterday's idea rather than today's. Time Warner, whose appetite for acquisitions was always greater than its capacity to finance or absorb them, made a deal too far and gave away half the company in exchange for AOL. And two European adventures in America have come to grief. Thomas Middelhoff was fired from Bertelsmann, Jean-Marie Messier from Vivendi, and the empires they built are being dismantled.

Although other media giants are in better shape, their experience does not offer strong support for the inevitable consolidation of the industry. News Corporation and Viacom are the creations of business geniuses with an exceptional eye for undervalued assets and the evolution of their industries. But with Rupert Murdoch 72 and Sumner Redstone 80, the future direction of these businesses is bound to change. Michael Eisner's vision for Disney was that you made money for Disney shareholders – and for Eisner himself – by exploiting the existing repertoire far more exhaustively than anyone had imagined possible.

The argument for vertical integration is that delivery needs content, and *vice versa*. This was why the AOL Time Warner deal was, briefly, thought to be a marriage made in heaven. Content does need delivery, but it does not need to own it; the *Financial Times* needs the newspaper delivery boy's bicycle, but does not need to buy it. The notion that Disney, with material to die for, required the ABC network to gain distribution for its product, was always ludicrous. And there are good arguments for keeping these businesses apart. The newspaper round will be more efficient if one bicycle carries several titles, and there will never be much rapport between a rap artist and a telephone company.

Perhaps horizontal integration is required by technological convergence, as new media blur traditional boundaries between print, film and music. But assembling disparate groups of people with past success in established production and distribution systems is not necessarily the best way to exploit these opportunities. Music publishers have been more concerned to defend their existing businesses against the internet than to exploit its opportunities. New thinking comes most often from new companies.

Some people emphasise the opportunities for cross selling in a multi-media business. Warner Bros can use AOL to promote Harry Potter movies on the internet. But you do not need common ownership for this, as the example illustrates. The originator of the Potter phenomenon is the independent book publisher Bloomsbury (which perceived the potential the conglomerates had missed) and subsidiary rights are licensed to many different companies. Books with television tie-ins are today's fashion, but it is only fortuitous if the network and the publisher are part of the same corporation.

Media conglomerates are the product of the ambitions of those who run them rather than the imperatives of the market. Media businesses depend on talented, often difficult, individuals, and their well-founded suspicion of large multinationals is a major obstacle to the success of such businesses. The low risk bureaucratic way to run a media company is to focus on products very similar to those which have already succeeded. And you need only look at television, music and films today to see that this is exactly what happens.

Today's bestseller list consists of books you have already read: diet guides, courtroom thrillers and sporting biographies. I counted three genuinely original works among them: *The Life of Pi, The Number One Ladies Detective Agency,* and *Schott's Miscellany*. Each was brought to market by a small, independent, specialist publisher.

Retailing

5 MARCH 1996

Retailing exists because consumers are ignorant, small, and immobile. When I plan tonight's supper, my first problem is that I do not know the range of options available. Nor, within that range, do I know what is good and what is not. I ask the retailer to search and select on my behalf.

Having decided on beans, I face my second problem. I am small. It is difficult for me to negotiate a good price against the might of Heinz and the power of Crosse and Blackwell. The retailer aggregates the demands of many potential customers and bargains on behalf of us all.

And then I find it inconvenient to visit the Heinz factory to collect my beans. My third problem is my immobility. I would rather pick up the beans from some more convenient location, close to home, and ideally with a car park.

Retailing exists to solve these three problems. The three components of retailing are product search and selection, purchasing, and delivery logistics. In grocery distribution, all these functions have come together – Sainsbury and Tesco do them all. That was not true thirty years ago. There are some markets in which a different agent performs each of these three functions, like pharmaceuticals. That doesn't sound like a system that will last. And there are other industries which sell to final customers, like financial services and travel, which have yet to organise themselves on these functional lines.

So where does electronic home shopping fit into this picture? It doesn't resolve the problem that I'm small. And it doesn't help much with the logistics either. There are one or two products that you can send down a wire into people's homes, like videos and banking services, but no technology yet devised can deliver a can of beans or a washing machine on the internet.

The service of electronic ordering of food shopping has existed for a long time. It used to be called ringing up the grocer, who would send his delivery boy round on a bicycle. It is a service that largely disappeared, because it costs too much to provide. And nothing has changed that basic economics.

What modern technology offers that is new is a capacity for structured search – the capacity to interrogate the electronic media to search for the goods and services you want. New technology may not resolve the problem that I'm small, or deliver the product: but it helps reduce my ignorance, or at least helps me to organise it.

The functions of retailing

Customer Problem	Business Function	Who deals with problem	
		Food	Pharmaceuticals
Ignorant	Search & selection	Retailer	Doctor
Small	Bargaining & purchasing	Retailer	NHS/Benefit manager
Immobile	Distribution logistics	Retailer	Pharmacy

So the ideal product for electronic shopping is the washing machine, a product sufficiently complicated and sufficiently expensive to justify an effective search across the available product range, and too big and bulky to be taken home by the shopper.

And yet people could buy washing machines today off the catalogue or on the phone. But mostly they don't. What they actually do is rather peculiar. They visit a display of washing machines. All machines look virtually identical, and they sit in the middle of the shop floor, devoid of plumbing or electricity, like beached whales. If you asked the assistants to demonstrate them for you, they would assume you were off your head. All you get from the display is the reassurance of the physical presence of the machine. You can touch it, you can feel it. One way or another that seems to be very important. Maybe virtual reality can deliver the same reassurance. Somehow I doubt it.

What really drives changes in market and industry structure is not simply the availability of technology, but changes in the underlying economic and commercial structures. Remember again that retailing exists because consumers are small, ignorant and immobile. And that group of problems applies to almost everything we buy. Yet what is retailed amounts to little more than half of consumer expenditure.

The other half of what we spend is varied. It includes housing, utilities, financial products, petrol, and many kinds of services – cleaning, car maintenance, conveyancing. There is scope for retailing almost all of these: providing the combination of search and selection, effective purchasing, and convenient distribution logistics which are characteristic of those retailing activities that already exist.

You can already see this happening. Supermarkets have captured a quarter of the petrol market, you can make withdrawals from your bank account from a machine on their sites or through their tills, and Marks & Spencer will make you a loan or sell you a mutual fund. As competition comes to utility markets, a surprising range of companies will emerge as suppliers of gas and electricity. And why can't the house shop take over from the estate agent and the money shop from the bank? Some of these new retailers will be physical shops like those we are used to, others virtual shops at the end of the telephone. That half of consumer expenditure that is retailed could rise to three quarters. There is a lot of scope there for a very different industrial structure to the one we know today.

Going global

6 OCTOBER 1997

The world market for accountancy has become polarised around six firms, American or Anglo-American in origin, operating worldwide. Does this mean that the number will inevitably reduce to five, to four and ultimately to one? Or that the same sort of polarisation will inevitably happen in investment banking, law, publishing, telecommunications and aviation?

Similar trends will emerge in some of these industries, although not all. If they do emerge, they will have quite different origins and rationale. The validity of analogies depends on specific common features of the industries compared, not on generalisations about historic inevitability.

The meaning of globalisation differs from industry to industry. There is a difference between globalisation for Boeing, which produces for the world market from a single Seattle location, and globalisation for Ernst and Young, which attaches an international brand to local output. Investment banks are like Boeing, and hotel chains are like Ernst and Young. The model of centralised production is driven by economies of scale, and the model of international branding by the hesitations of customers who need to buy in unfamiliar environments.

So there are no local manufacturers of jumbo jets but – since hesitant cross-border purchasers of accountancy and hotel rooms are only a part of the market – there are many successful small local accountants and hoteliers. Even these analogies need to be unpicked carefully. Access to capital markets involves scale economies, which is why that side of the investment banking business is becoming more concentrated and global. But investment banks also act as financial consultants, and there are no scale economies in that. So smaller boutiques will thrive: large and small investment banks will just do different things.

Nor does the removal of trade barriers necessarily lead to bigger firms: only to industries based on competitive advantage rather than national preference. The growth of international trade and competition in automobiles benefited BMW and Honda as it damaged General Motors and Ford. In telecommunications and aviation, restrictions which once aligned the boundaries of firms with the boundaries of nations are fast disappearing. But it is not obvious what follows from that. The rise of Southwest Airlines and EasyJet, of Kallback and Orange, may be more significant pointers to the ways these industries will evolve than BT's uneasy global relationship in Concert.

How industry structures evolve depends, therefore, on specifics of technology and conditions of supply and demand. Audit – the product which remains the direct and indirect key to the profitability of accounting firms – is a very particular commodity. You buy audit only because others require it of you, and your incentive is to buy the minimum that satisfies these requirements.

This need for certification explains why accountancy is characterised by tiers of firms with little to differentiate firms without the tiers. You can choose between Price and Young, Peat and Touche, Deloitte and Waterhouse, confident that each can do the job, and perceiving no need to have more than the job done. And since audit is a function placed by the corporate head office, you want to entrust it to a single firm with global reach. Preferably one with a principal office in London or New York, the cities with the largest concentrations of corporate head offices.

But that particular combination of factors does not apply to any other industry. Insurance broking probably comes closest. Even law – an industry obsessed by the accounting analogy – is very different. The distinction between the best and the good matters far more in law than in audit. And while there are some areas of legal practice – like multinational acquisitions – for which a centrally controlled process is necessary and appropriate, there are many areas of law for which this is not true. Law is and will remain less international and less concentrated than accountancy: major law firms will continue to be much more differentiated from each other than major accountancy firms: and why the profitability of law firms is based not on size but on specialist skills. The most lucrative legal services businesses – tiny measured by their share of the world legal services market – are the specialist chambers of leading commercial barristers.

Ambitious managers are so anxious to believe that all business is becoming larger and more international that everything is assumed to point in that direction. Yet if the changes in technology which increase scale economies in investment banking and aviation point towards greater concentration, it can hardly be true that the changes in technology which reduce scale economies in publishing and telecommunications have the same effect. The point is not that there are no valid generalisations about business, but that no valid generalisations about business are independent of facts about different industries.

The 'big six' accounting firms reduced to five following the merger of Price Waterhouse Coopers and to four after the disintegration of Arthur Andersen following the Enron scandal. It is likely that regulation will prevent any further consolidation.

The quest for value

If you turn to the index of Michael Porter's *Competitive Advantage*, you won't find the word profit there. The essays here deal with the links between the competitive advantage of the firm and its financial performance. The first part of this section describes how value is generated, and introduces the concept of economic rent – the differential profit derived from distinctive capabilities. The corollary is that distinctive capabilities are the only means by which businesses add value. The second part of this section is concerned to demolish the notion that sustained value can be created through varieties of financial engineering.

Principles of valuation

29 SEPTEMBER 1999

The Forth Bridge is a marvel of Victorian engineering. But few trains use it today. If it did not exist, it would not be built. Its value is far below its replacement cost. I cannot imagine life without a car: its value is inestimable. Yet when my insurance company asks its value, the figure I give is the replacement cost. Britain's Central Electricity Generating Board, before privatisation, put the value of its assets at £30bn, a measure of what it would cost to rebuild them today. When the company was sold, the flotation price for the two main successor companies was around £4bn.

One key principle unites these three examples. The economic value of an asset is the lower of the net present value of its earnings (the earnings basis) and the replacement cost (the replacement basis).

The earnings basis cannot generally exceed the replacement basis for long, because replacement basis is the price of entering the market. If newcomers can earn more than that price, entry will drive down earnings. Prudence therefore suggests that replacement cost is the appropriate valuation basis. If earnings are less than replacement cost, the assets are not worth what they cost to replace, and they will not normally be replaced. Prudence now suggests that earnings, not replacement cost, define the asset's value.

These mechanisms can be easily observed in businesses where there are ready markets for assets, such as ships and aircraft. Sometimes there is a glut and prices fall below replacement cost. Then orders are cancelled, and prices remain low until the surplus is scrapped. But prices rarely rise above replacement cost for long. These high prices stimulate new construction until value again reflects the costs.

Similar principles of valuation apply not just to physical assets, but to whole firms. The cost of reproducing an established, successful firm is generally very high. To replicate Barclays Bank, you would need to reproduce two hundred years of history. At first sight, the cost of replacing Coca-Cola would seem relatively modest: but the mistake is to confuse replicating the company with replicating the tangible assets of the company. The reality is that you could not replicate Coca-Cola however much you spent: after all, Pepsi has been trying for decades. Both Barclays Bank and Coca-Cola should be valued by reference to their earnings.

We find a different situation when we turn to Lastminute.com. the aptly named internet stock whose impending flotation by Morgan Stanley was announced recently. Lastminute.com was founded last April by two young entrepreneurs. Lastminute.com provides a website which allows buyers and sellers of last-minute services, such as vacant seats on package holidays, to be brought together. But if we ask what is the replacement cost of this admirable facility, the answer is a good deal lower than the £400 million valuation which has allegedly been attributed to it. Despite the extravagant earnings projections issued by the company's promoters, the value of the firm is capped by its replacement cost.

The same analysis can be applied to more substantive businesses. Take One2One, the smallest of the four British mobile telephone companies recently purchased by Deutsche Telekom for £8.4 billion. You can build the infrastructure to provide national mobile phone coverage across Britain for around a billion pounds. One2One has more than 2.5 million subscribers. This is an impressive number. But the cost of obtaining a subscriber in industries such as this – through a sales force or incentives – is typically £100–£200. The replacement cost of One2One's customer base would therefore be somewhere in the range £250m–£500m.

On the most extravagant assumptions, it is hard to put the cost of replicating One2One at more than a quarter of the price Deutsche Telekom paid. The reality check of replacement cost introduces competitive dynamics into earnings projections. If valuations based on anticipated earnings are so far above replacement cost, entry and rivalry will force these earnings down. (As a matter of fact, One2One has yet to make a profit.) True, there are only four British mobile networks, but there will be more, and the expansion from two to four has already brought lower prices. Internet advertising and mobile telephony are both wonderful businesses, but that alone ensures that their future will be fiercely competitive.

The current emphasis on earnings projections and neglect of replacement cost is sometimes justified by a belief that replacement cost is irrelevant: the first entrant to a market enjoys all the benefits of its subsequent growth. Experience of business history is entirely otherwise. If this theory were true, General Motors and Toyota would not be leaders among many automobile companies, Tesco and Sainsbury would not be leaders among many British food retailers, and Philip Morris would not be leader among several tobacco companies.

Almost all markets quickly become competitive – market leadership goes to those who enjoy competitive advantages – and high profits are the result, not of market expansion as such, but of strong and sustainable competitive advantages. Whatever else happens in the New Economy, the basic laws of market economics remain unchanged.

Lastminute.com was successfully floated at a price which valued the business at around £400m, and the offer was greatly oversubscribed. The share price quickly fell far below this level and never regained it. Deutsche Telekom remains the owner of One2One (later renamed T-Mobile) and no objective valuation of its business is available, but the shares of its principal quoted competitor, Vodafone, have fallen by more than two-thirds since this article was first published.

Do the math

24 APRIL 2000

'Do the math'. The slogan comes from Jim Clark, creator of Silicon Graphics, Netscape and Healtheon. It has become the mantra of a generation of consultants and investment bankers. The new economy, they claim, requires new principles of valuation.

C.com is one of the most exciting prospects in B2B commerce. It is the worldwide leader in a growing market – annual sales by 2010 are likely to be around $500 trillion. If C.com can maintain a 5% market share, and earn only 1% net margin, its prospective annual earnings are $250bn. If we assume that market growth after 2010 is 5% and discount future revenues at 10%, then the prospective value of C.com is $5000bn – around ten times the recent market capitalisation of Microsoft, Cisco or General Electric.

You don't even have to wait for the IPO. You can buy shares in C.com right now for less than 5% of that value. C.com is called Citigroup, and in addition to its foreign exchange trading, which is the business I have described, you get its wholesale, retail and investment banking activities and a leading insurance company thrown in for free.

Of course, nobody would be so stupid as to value Citigroup in this way. Still, I have followed more or less exactly the methodology recommended in the latest McKinsey quarterly for the valuation of new era companies. The authors (Desmet *et al.*) employ precisely analogous calculations to arrive at a valuation of $37bn for Amazon.com.

Paul Gibbs, head of merger and acquisition research at JPMorgan, recently used similar principles to confirm that assessment of Amazon. He goes on to do the same calculation for internet service provider Freeserve. Assume that UK retail sales grow at 5% a year, that 25% of sales take place on the net, that portals capture 50% of these, that Freeserve gets 30% of the portal share, and that Freeserve maintains an 8% commission on sales. Multiply all these numbers together and you establish that in 2017 Freeserve will make profits of £2bn. This, he argues, justifies a market value today of £6.50 per share.

But I prefer T.com to Freeserve. T.com has a customer base four times larger than Freeserve. Its franchise is much stronger, too. Its customers are concentrated in the affluent South-East of England, where it faces virtually no competition. Market research shows that more than 95% of its customers use its services – which are essential – every day, and many of them buy several times a day.

Moreover, T.com has ambitious plans for expansion. At present, its geographical coverage is less than one quarter of the market in England and Wales. T.com has a particular interest in South East Asia. The population of China is one hundred times the number of people who today can access T.com services. Even after the recent market correction, T.com, better known as Thames Water, still has a market valuation below that of Freeserve. At the height of the new economy boom, Freeserve was worth four times as much.

The reason the Citibank calculation is nonsense is simple, but fundamental. The margins Citibank makes on its forex business vary widely. If you buy small quantities of notes from a bank branch, the spread is much wider than 1%. If you are a large corporation trading major currencies, then the margin is wafer thin. Entry and competition force prices in each line of business down to the related costs.

In Mr Gibbs' model, Freeserve earns profits of £2bn – about equal to the current profits of Tesco, Sainsbury and Marks & Spencer together. And it earns these profits on revenues of only £2.5bn, so that profits are 80% of the value of its sales. No established business earns margins of that size. And for good reasons. If competition doesn't get you, competition authorities will.

Thames Water is one of a very small number of companies whose market position is so strong, whose output is so necessary to everyday life, that if it charged five times the cost of the services it provides we would have few options but to pay. Still, we do have one option, which is to insist that the government intervenes. And a pretty effective option it is too. It confines Thames Water to a return on its capital employed of around 6%.

The old-fashioned idea that profit is a return on capital invested still has some role in new economy valuation, at the level of the overall market. There is a key formula in the new math. The required yield on a security is equal to the difference between the rate of return demanded from that class of securities and its expected rate of growth. So if you expect a return of 5.5% from a share whose dividends will grow at 5%, the dividend yield on it should be 0.5%.

This is exactly the calculation done by Glassman and Hassett in their recent book *Dow* 36,000. Claiming that sustainable dividends average half of earnings, this yield equates to a market price earnings ratio of 100. That in turn implies a target of 36,000 for the American index.

Investors buying at this level will need to be extremely patient. Only 40% of the cash that sustains the valuation will accrue this century. And one third of it depends on dividend cheques that will be arriving after the year 2200. The Dow Jones index had not been established two hundred years ago. We can visualise the businesses a prudent, diversified investor would then have owned: slave traders and sugar plantations. He might have made a bold speculation in that symbol of the then new economy – the canal.

Perhaps the next 200 years will be more stable than the last, and perhaps Microsoft and Cisco will prove more enduring businesses than canals and plantations. But we can hardly be sure. While 5% may be a reasonable assumption for the growth rate of dividends in the US economy as a whole, it is likely that well before 2200 most of these dividends will come from companies that have not yet been founded – like Microsoft and Cisco only two decades ago.

The rules of logic hold even in cyberspace, and so do the principles of economics. Profits are hard to earn in competitive businesses, and markets that are not competitive are usually regulated. The value of companies ultimately depends on their capacity to generate cash for their shareholders. Distant returns are uncertain. Share prices are very volatile, and investors need to be compensated for the associated risks. These simple truths are as valid in the new economy as the old.

By all means do the math. Isaac Newton, who could do the math better than anyone else in history, gave up an annuity of £650 per year to invest in the South Sea Bubble. In addition to the math, you need the econ, the pol, and perhaps the psychology.

Amazon.com is today capitalised at around £20bn. Freeserve was acquired by France Telecom in December 2000 for 157p per share. Lastminute.com used the cash it obtained at flotation to purchase other travel agencies. In 2005 it was bought by a US company for about half the original flotation price.

Cost and competitive advantage

21 AUGUST 2003

Could so much of industry really have been so inefficient? That question puzzled me a decade ago. Chief executives with one eye on the bottom line and another on their share options could tell their subordinates to cut costs. And in almost every line of business these subordinates could do it.

A conversation with a friend who worked in the water industry supplied the answer. He explained that most of the people who worked in his company were there to stop things going wrong, or to fix them once they had. There was no scientific way of judging whether there was too much inspection or too little.

In his business, planning followed a regulatory cycle. The regulator would require cost savings at each review, and the company would then find a bit more to keep the stock market happy. And this was always possible. If you fired all the operating employees, then costs would plummet but the water would keep flowing.

That couldn't go on for ever, of course. And as we talked, we saw an inevitable future. There would be an unpleasant incident: customers would be poisoned, or there would be extended disruption of supply. People would point to things that could have been done, but hadn't been. And then, in panic, money would be thrown at the industry to ensure there was no repetition. It wouldn't be well spent.

We described the process completely accurately, we just got the industry wrong. It didn't happen in the British water industry – although it still might. It happened instead on Britain's railways. And now it has happened in the American electricity industry.*

We all want pure water and reliable electricity, we want our trains to be both punctual and safe, but you can always make the water even purer and the electricity more reliable if you spend a bit more. A balance has to be struck, and finding that balance demands fine, and debatable, judgment. Public sector managers made cautious assessments. Private sector executives were more inclined to be optimistic. No-one can say, with confidence, who was right and who was wrong. But British rail commuters and New York electricity consumers may be forgiven for judging – after the event – that their suppliers made mistakes.

The consequences of utility failures are obvious, and unacceptable. But they only exemplify what has happened across large sectors of British and American industry in the last decade. We now recognise the dishonest ways in which companies inflated their current earnings at the expense of their assets – as at Enron and WorldCom. What is emerging only more slowly is the honest ways in which other companies inflated their current earnings at the expense of their assets.

This was possible because modern business depends on intangible factors which, for good reasons, are not measured in the balance sheet. Security of supply is one. But the loyalty of employees, the trust of customers, and the quality of service are also assets that require investment and depreciate if not well maintained.

But since the assets are not measured, reducing investment in them enhances current earnings. Media companies could focus on producing clones of already successful works, and it would be a few years before their bored audiences turned away. Financial institutions could replace their customer service staff by sales people and call centres. Drug companies could reduce costs and obtain synergies through merger – and today find their pipelines of new drugs thinner than they have ever been.

Actions have consequences. And when revenues slowed, it was possible to restore earnings with another round of cost reductions. 'Disappointing results mean more job cuts' has been a staple FT headline for a decade. These companies are engaged in a process of internal liquidation. Eventually they will have cut out everything that made people want to do business with them.

In media, pharmaceuticals and finance, businesses which have funded the present at the expense of the future will continue to decline, and others will take their place. But there is no similar market solution for infrastructure utilities. Determining the right balance between supply security and costs will always be a matter of expert regulatory judgment and political negotiation. The illusion of the last two decades was that it could ever be otherwise.

---

* In August 2003 there were extensive blackouts in the north-eastern United States.

Business heroes

DR ATKINS

18 FEBRUARY 2004

Dr Robert Atkins (1930–2003) graduated from Cornell Medical School in 1955. In 1972 he published *Dr Atkins Diet Revolution*, supporting a low carbohydrate, high protein diet which enjoyed a brief vogue. A new version published twenty years later, supported by aggressive advertising and self-promotion, became a bestseller: but it was after a *New York Times* magazine article by Gary Tankes that the Atkins diet became the most popular diet of all time. In 2003 Dr Atkins fell in a New York street and subsequently died in hospital. The fad faded, as fads do, and in 2005 the Atkins Corporation filed for Chapter 11 protection. The American Heart Association has stated that 'high protein diets are not recommended because they restrict healthful foods that provide essential nutrients and do not provide the variety of foods needed to adequately meet nutritional needs'.

Was the late Dr Atkins really morbidly obese? Or was he merely slightly overweight when he fell over in the street and died? Whatever the answer, the doctor's career is a more powerful tribute to the power of modern marketing than to the capacity of his nostrums to prolong life.

The Atkins diet restricts carbohydrate intake. It works, up to a point, because we use carbohydrates as a source of energy and, when deprived of them, dip into reserves of accumulated fat. The process of burning fat produces ketones which some claim have an appetite-suppressing effect. But if we go for long without nutrition, we die, just as an aircraft which is running on its emergency gasoline supplies ultimately falls out of the sky.

Eventually, you need to start refuelling. At that point, you discover that the only way to achieve a healthy lifestyle is to rethink your eating habits and adopt a balanced diet involving moderate quantities of varied foods. You always knew that, of course, but like me and millions of other people, you hoped that if you bought a diet book the weight would magically slip away.

The model of fuel supplies supplemented by replenishable reserves is common not just in biological systems, but in economic and social ones. We keep capital in our businesses for the same reason as we collect fat around our bottoms: to keep us going through an interruption in the supply of cash (in one case) or carbohydrates (in the other). We build up goodwill with customers and employees in the hope that we can rely on their loyalty in hard times.

As these analogies show, we are not fat because nature wants us to be ugly. Fat has a biological purpose: for most of history fat was a sign of prosperity and rich men were proud of their rotund wives – look at the ideal of human beauty in a Rubens painting. On the savannahs where our genetic inheritance was determined, food supplies were sometimes scarce. That is why we are programmed to eat what is put in front of us, even airline meals. But in the twenty-first century we can remedy nutritional deficiency immediately with a call to a pizza delivery service.

With pizza cheap, and health clubs expensive, it is now more costly to be thin than to be fat. But our metabolisms have not yet adjusted to this modern environment.

The business environment has experienced similar changes. Globalisation has made markets more responsive and flexible. Our companies, like our bodies, have less need of self sufficiency. Just-in-time management is the commercial equivalent of dialling for a pizza. Healthy businesses used to display their fat with the same exuberance: banks would impress their depositors with marble banking halls. Woolworth and Chrysler, Unilever and ICI built head offices that were testimonials to their wealth and permanence. But the corporations of today are abandoning these edifices. Cutting out the fat, becoming lean and mean, are now commercial clichés.

So doing an Atkins is now fashionable in business as in personal life. But in business – as on the female body – there are places where you want fat as well as those where you do not. It is one thing to slim an overstaffed activity, another to burn the loyalty of your employees. Ketosis reduces fat indiscriminately, and so do many cost reduction programmes.

But the larger issue is sustainability. Atkins is effective at short-term weight loss, as slash and burn managers are effective at short-term earnings growth. And business consultants and market analysts fulfil the role of the ketones – they let you feel good about your diet, and convince you that you can continue indefinitely. But you can't. Both weight loss and the earnings growth are limited by the available fat. Its depletion leaves your body craving food and your customers craving nourishment.

Burning fat is the right emergency treatment for the morbidly obese – in life or in business. But good nutrition demands a balanced diet, and good business a balanced scorecard. The healthiest bodies – those of athletes and soldiers – soak up carbohydrates and use the energy they yield productively. It is to their lifestyle, not that of Dr Atkins, that we should look for business analogies.

Business heroes

JOHN MAYO

29 JANUARY 2002

As an investment banker at SG Warburg, John Mayo advised ICI on its response to a putative bid from Hanson and master-minded the demerger of the chemicals and pharmaceutical businesses. In 1992 he became finance director of Zeneca (the pharmaceutical subsidiary) and in 1997 joined GEC (subsequently renamed Marconi) as Finance Director. Marconi engaged in a spree of acquisitions and diversifications. In 2001 he was nominated as chief executive designate, but in early 2002 the company encountered severe financial difficulties. Mayo resigned. The company subsequently restructured its debts and disposed of its principal activities. A small successor business, Telent, continues to trade.

...il businesses are more effective than their competitors in ...ig goods and services that their customers want. They add value if their superior delivery enables them to command a premium price: or if they design their operations in such a way that they meet these needs at lower cost. The job of the corporate executive is to achieve these objectives.

These points seem so basic to any understanding of business that one feels embarrassed at writing them down. If they are worth repeating, it is as a reminder to those who have been reading John Mayo's account of his stewardship of Marconi in recent issues of the *Financial Times*.

Mr Mayo appears to have a quite different perception of his role, in which the director of a company is a meta-fund manager, managing a portfolio of businesses for his shareholders. His function differs from that of a fund manager only in that the fund manager buys and sells stakes in companies while the manager of the company buys and sells the companies themselves. And – as with a fund manager – the executive's job is to buy cheap and sell dear. He believes he should be judged on his success in doing that.

Since the costs of buying and selling companies are much higher than the costs of buying and selling shares in companies, great skill and fine judgment are required to make money in this way. Unfortunately for the shareholders of Marconi, Mr Mayo and his colleagues lacked those skills. They bought telecommunications companies at very high prices and they and their successors will have to sell them at lower ones. But the problem is not just that they did the job badly. It is the wrong job.

It has been said that the only reference to teaching in C.P. Snow's series of novels about Cambridge University is when one of the dons agrees to postpone a tutorial to enable him to devote more time to politicking. And Mr Mayo's attitude to the operational activities of the company of which he was a director is very similar. There are no references to products, customers or employees. Or even to profits, except in the context of managing stock market expectations.

Now, in Mr Mayo's defence, it must be acknowledged that he was the company's finance director: the bursar of the College rather than one of its tutors. But this is a weak defence. Even the most foolish bursar knows that finance is a function that makes the activities of the university possible, rather than the object of the university itself.

But Mr Mayo, and others who think like him, believe that business is different. The portfolio shift he masterminded was the company's central strategy. And Mr Mayo asserts that the measure of performance – the company's performance, not just the finance director's performance – should be the total shareholder return. He devotes a lot of space to an elaborate calculation of that measure.

The paradox to which this gives rise is found in Mr Mayo's description of his principal disagreement with his boardroom colleagues. In February 2000, he explains, it was obvious to him, as to others, that telecoms stocks were overvalued. At that point, he concluded, the right thing to do was to sell the company. His logic is impeccable. But the conclusion to which it leads is so absurd that he could not bring his fellow directors to agree with it. Even more absurd is the lesson he draws – that you should never buy a business without an agreed exit strategy. Sensible advice to a fund manager. Ludicrous advice to a businessman, dependent on the continuing loyalty of customers and staff.

If Mr Mayo had been a fund manager, rather than the finance director of Marconi, his recommendation to sell Marconi shares would have been appropriate and well timed. But a company director is not a fund manager. His job is to run a business that adds value by means of the services it provides to its customers. If he succeeds, it will generate returns to investors in the long-term. And this is the only mechanism that can generate returns to investors in the long-term.

The problem is that the equivalence between value added in operations and stock market returns holds in the long run but not the short. Share prices may, for a time, become divorced from the fundamental value of a business. This has been true of most share prices in recent years and was true of the Marconi share price throughout Mr Mayo's tenure. In these conditions, attention to total shareholder return distracts executives from their real function of managing businesses. And their reactions in fact reduce the ability of the corporate sector as a whole even to generate total shareholder returns on a sustainable basis. This is the price we pay for the hyperactive capital markets of recent years.

What a fund manager needs most is a bull market, and the meta-fund managers, such as Mr Mayo, did well in the great bull market of 1982–2000. Marconi, Enron and Swissair will not be the only businesses run in these ways that will come to grief as the rising tide that once raised all boats gradually ebbs. Perhaps we shall move into an age in which senior executives again understand that managing companies is not about mergers, acquisitions and disposals, but about running operating businesses well. And that corporate strategy is about matching the capabilities of the business to the needs of its customers.

Morning coffee at Jenners

19 JULY 2005

House of Fraser has just announced the closure of Dickins & Jones, the department store which has occupied a prime position on Regent Street for over a century.

This story seems to have been developing all my life. As a boy in Edinburgh, I was dragged by my mother round the department stores for which the city was renowned. On Princes Street were Binns, Smalls and Jenners: you turned the corner into North Bridge and found Patrick Thomson and J. & R. Allan. One by one, these shops were bought by House of Fraser.

Customers were fiercely loyal to their favourite store. Old Edinburgh hands could distinguish a Smalls client from a J. & R. Allan shopper at a glance. But they would begin muttering that 'Patrick Thomson is not what it was'. Then the store would close. Today only Binns, trading as Frasers, and Jenners, whose founding family were determined to keep the shop out of Fraser's clutches, are left.

Even as a boy, I did not understand how acquisition followed by closure was a smart business strategy. Some people said that the era of the large department store was over, others that the wily Fraser was set on achieving a retail monopoly. But both accounts were refuted by the arrival of new retailers – Debenhams, John Lewis and ultimately Harvey Nichols – to fill the market slots vacated when Fraser shops shut. Still, I was told, in the Scottish phrase, to haud my wheesh: Lord Fraser of Allander, as he became, was the greatest Scottish businessman of the age, the draper's assistant who had risen to be proprietor of Harrods, the world's most famous emporium.

The rags to riches account was exaggerated. Although Fraser had begun his working life behind the counter, his promotion at the age of twenty-one to managing director of a chain of stores owed less to his undoubted talents than to his father's position as owner of the company. But Fraser had been among the first to see the potential gains from arbitrage between equity markets and property markets. He had used sale and leaseback deals to release cash for acquisitions, successively repeating the process until he reached Central London.

But, as on the first day of Harrods sale, the bargains amongst department stores were quickly snapped up. In some early transactions Fraser did acquire retail brands for less than the value of the underlying property assets – as Charles Clore would also do in southern England. But later deals involved substantial acquisition premia. The goodwill thus purchased proved ephemeral when, as Fraser retreated from the business, the effectiveness of its management declined.

The attempt to add value to retailing through financial engineering gained sophistication. Lloyds Bank would show how raising the return on equity through sale and leaseback allowed you to use highly valued paper, rather than cash, as currency for acquisitions. Private equity firms would reduce the cost of capital by confusing investors with multiple layers of debt. Today they cluster round the retailing sector like – well, locusts.

But, as the sad experience of Edinburgh's House of Fraser stores demonstrated, you can only create enterprise value in the long run by better management of the operating business. And since all finance houses are drawing from the same limited pool of retailing expertise, there is simply not enough better management to go round. Too often, banks have been repaid from the proceeds of the closing down sale. Patrick Thomson is not what it was, then Patrick Thomson is no more. This happened equally at Whiteleys, Gamages and now Dickins & Jones.

The small boy who did not understand Fraser's business strategy, the ladies who regretted the deterioration of their favourite store, were closer to the heart of the matter than the advisers who structured Fraser's deals.

But what goes around comes around. Even as House of Fraser announced the final markdowns at Dickins & Jones, the company achieved the prize that had eluded its founders. Jenners failed to recognise that the daughters of ladies who had met there for morning coffee now worked in Edinburgh's growing finance and government sectors, and shopped at lunchtime in Harvey Nichols. And so the most famous of Princes Street stores has just become part of House of Fraser.

Business heroes

AL DUNLAP (2)

7 JUNE 2005

In 1996 Dunlap (p. 85) was appointed Chief Executive of
Sunbeam. He was dismissed by the Board two years later. In
February 2001, Sunbeam filed for bankruptcy protection under
Chapter 11. The Securities and Exchange Commission charged
that Dunlap had been 'engaged in a fraudulent scheme to create
the illusion of a successful restructuring at Sunbeam'. He paid
$15 million to settle a class action suit by Sunbeam
stockholders, and was fined $500,000 by the SEC and accepted
a ban from working as officer or director of a public company.

Can or must the obligations of directors to their company be translated into an obligation to achieve the highest possible price for the company's stock?

The problems entailed in such a view have never been better illustrated than by the chaotic reign of Al Dunlap, arch-champion of shareholder value, and one-time chief executive of Sunbeam Corporation, providers of toasters, mixers and blenders to generations of Americans. The agreement that took the business out of chapter 11 bankruptcy left stockholders, whom Dunlap described in his tract *Mean Business* as 'the only constituency I am concerned about', with nothing at all.

The longest chapter of that book is entitled 'Impressing the analysts'. It records Dunlap telling a group of fund managers 'we will be successful because I say we will be.' The remark was greeted, he notes modestly, with 'enthusiastic shouting and applause'. Such exchanges are a powerful means of creating shareholder value. But not of building businesses.

The price of a company's stock depends, not on the value of a company, but on the market's perception of that value, which is often easier to change than the value itself. Dunlap's relentless self-promotion, and his purported emphasis on the primacy of shareholder interests, influenced perceptions. The mere announcement that he was taking the helm at Sunbeam almost doubled the company's stock price. At its peak, barely three months before Dunlap was fired as the company fell to pieces, Sunbeam's market value had increased fivefold since his appointment. Stock prices reflect underlying realities in the long run, but even at Sunbeam, the five years from Dunlap's appointment to corporate collapse were longer than the 'long run' of most executive incentive schemes.

Market values respond more immediately to reported earnings than to business fundamentals. But there are many ways to manage earnings short of the outright fraud at WorldCom and the artificial schemes of Enron. Sunbeam filled warehouses with product and booked the revenues. Whether or not this was legal depends on the fine detail of the contracts, but the business consequence of such a manoeuvre is to bring profits into the current quarter at the cost of an equal or greater subsequent reduction in later reporting periods. Other measures, such as scaling back development and postponing maintenance expenditures, raise no legal or accounting issues but have the same effect. They boost profit but reduce value.

Some people still believe – against all evidence – that the market is generally successful in obtaining a clear view of a company's real performance through the rose-tinted lenses provided even by reputable finance directors. But judging the quality of a manager by his effect on the stock price is exactly equivalent to judging a weather forecaster on whether you like what they tell you.

Chief executives largely paid in stock options may understandably check their company's share price several times a day, but it is extraordinary that some of them believe that by doing so they gain information about their business. Anyone tempted to think this should remember the fate of Chainsaw Al. Or that of Bernie Ebbers, WorldCom chairman, whose familiar routine was to point to a chart of the stock price and ask fawning analysts for questions. Where business judgment and market judgment differ, the responsibility of managers is to implement their business judgment.

And since it is for their business judgment that they are hired, it is for their business judgment, not for their ability to generate 'enthusiastic shooting and applause', that executives should be rewarded. Managers whose attention is closely focused on the stock price – whether by their inclination or because they have incentives to do so – will often fail to serve the best interests even of their stockholders.

The goal

An overview of strategy

27 SEPTEMBER 1999

It is the early 1960s. Robert Macnamara, recruited from Ford to run the Department of Defense, is managing the first stages of the Vietnam War by computers in the Pentagon. John Kenneth Galbraith, detesting the world Macnamara represents, writes of the New Industrial State, in which giant mechanistic corporations run our lives.

The Soviet Union is ahead in the space race and while most of the West loathes the Russian empire, few dispute the claims made for its economic success. Every newly independent colonial territory looks forward to the realisation of its development plan. The British Prime Minister, Harold Wilson, talks of the white heat of the technological revolution, while his deputy George Brown gives Britain its first, and only, national plan.

In this environment the concept of business strategy enters the vocabulary of senior executives and MBA students. The early texts are by Igor Ansoff and Ken Andrews. The principal journal of the subject is called Long Range Planning. The subject of strategy is founded on an illusion of rationality and the possibilities of control. As the decade ends, this world will fall apart. Macnamara will be translated to the World Bank, and history will ultimately note the failure of each of his careers – as business executive, politician, and international statesman. Half a million hippies will gather at Woodstock to celebrate the demise of the New Industrial State – and – although few people saw it then – the Soviet Union is on an unstoppable path from totalitarianism to disintegration.

Yet the illusion of control has continued to define the subject of business strategy. In the heady 1960s, no major firm was without its strategic plan. Few are without them today, although few devote the resources to them they once did. They contain numbers, neither targets nor forecasts, which purport to describe the evolution of the company's affairs over the next five years.

But planning and strategy are no longer conflated. The illusion of control has changed its form if not its nature. What matters today are vision and mission. Charismatic CEOs can transcend the boundaries of the firm. Their achievements, and those of the companies they inspire, are restricted only by the limitations of the imagination.

But businesses are not defined by the imagination of their executives. They are limited by their own capabilities, by technology, by competition, and by the demands of their customers. And visionary strategy has been succeeded by an era in which the cliché 'formulation is easy, it is implementation that's the problem' holds sway. If strategising consists of having visions, it is obvious that formulation is easy and implementation the problem: all substantive issues of strategy have been redefined as issues of implementation. As organisations stubbornly fail to conform to the visions of their senior executives, we should not be surprised that organisational transformation has become one of the most popular branches of consultancy.

Sometimes the vision of the CEO is of the external environment, rather than the internal capabilities of the firm. The future belongs to those who see it first, or most clearly. But this is rarely true. Forecasting is hard. The inadequacy of this approach is more fundamental. Even if you do see the future correctly, its timing is hard to predict and its implications are uncertain.

AT&T, the US telecoms carrier, understood that the convergence of telecommunications and computing would transform not only the company's own markets but much of business life. It was a perceptive vision, not widely shared. But the company failed to see – how could it have? – that the internet was the specific vehicle through which the vision would be realised, and that its merger with NCR, the US business machines manufacturer, was an irrelevant and inappropriate response. There are many examples – take General Motors or IBM – of companies which suffered from failing to see the future even after it had arrived. There are almost none of companies building sustainable competitive advantages from superior forecasting abilities.

Thoughtful strategy, then, is not about crystal balls, or grand designs and visions. The attempt to formulate grand designs for national economies is now seen to have been at best ineffective and at worst disastrous – with Soviet economic planning, Mao's Cultural Revolution, and the development strategies of almost all developing countries. What has been true of states is true also in companies. No one has, or could hope to have, the knowledge necessary to construct these transformational plans. Nor, however totalitarian the structures they introduce – in governments or corporations – does anyone truly enjoy the power to implement them.

★ ★ ★

Business strategy is concerned with the match between the internal capabilities of the company and its external environment. Although there is much disagreement of substance among those who write about strategy, most agree this is the issue.

The methods of strategy, and its central questions, follow from that definition. The methods require analysis of the characteristics of the company and the industries and markets in which it operates. And that leads directly to two groups of question. What are the origins and characteristics of the successful fit between characteristics and environment? Why do companies succeed? How can companies and their managers make that fit more effective? How will companies succeed?

I once thought that these core issues of strategy – the positive question of understanding the processes through which effective strategies had been arrived at, the normative question of what effective strategy should be – were quite separate. I now believe they are barely worth distinguishing, and that this view of strategy formulation is the product of the illusion of control.

Strategy is not planning, visioning or forecasting – all remnants of the belief that one can control the future by superior insight and superior will. The modern subject of business strategy is a set of analytic techniques for understanding better, and so influencing, a company's position in its actual and potential marketplace.

★ ★ ★

Strategy, as I have defined it, is a subject of application, rather than a discipline – rather as, say, geriatrics is to underlying disciplines of pharmacology or cell biology – and the obvious underpinning disciplines for strategy are economics and organisational sociology. But this is not how the subject developed in practice.

When the content of strategy was first set out thirty years ago, industrial economics was dominated by the structure – conduct – performance paradigm, which emphasised how market structure – the number of competitors and the degree of rivalry between them – was the principal influence on a company's behaviour. Market structure was determined partly by external conditions of supply and demand, and partly (unless anti-trust-agencies intervened) by the attempts of firms to influence the intensity of competition.

This was a view of markets aimed at public policy, not business policy. And the microeconomic theory which resulted was correctly seen as having little relevance to the basic issues of business strategy. The neglect of the internal characteristics of companies is obvious and explicit. While some of the strategic tools developed by consultants in the 1970s – such as the experience curve and the portfolio matrix – might advantageously have had an economic basis, in practice microeconomic theory was largely ignored.

Not until 1980, with the publication of Michael Porter's *Competitive Strategy*, did economists attempt to recapture the field of strategy. But this would ultimately prove a false move. Porter's work – essentially a translation of the structure-conduct-performance paradigm into language more appropriate for a business audience – suffered from the limitations of the material on which it was based. Porter's 'five forces' and the value chain he identified five years later in *Competitive Advantage* are usefully descriptive of industry structure, but shed no light on the central strategic issue: why different firms, facing the same environment, perform differently.

Much of the organisational sociology of the 1960s examined strategic issues. Chandler's magisterial *Strategy and Structure*, or the empirical work of Tom Burns and G. M. Stalker, addressed directly the relationships between organisational form and the technological and market environment. But academic sociology was subsequently captured by people mostly hostile to the very concept of capitalist organisation. The subject drifted into abstraction, and further away from the day-to-day concerns of those in business.

More recent insights into the nature of organisations have come either from economics, as in the work of Paul Milgrom and John Roberts or from the accumulated practical wisdom of which Charles Handy and Henry Mintzberg are, in different ways, effective exponents. Porter's attention ultimately reverted to the public policy concerns of his former mentors in the Harvard economics department, as in *The Competitive Advantage of Nations*.

★ ★ ★

At about the same time as Porter first wrote about strategy, the *Strategic Management Journal*, today the leading journal in the field, was established. The currently dominant view of strategy – resource-based theory – has been principally set out in its pages.

Just as the 'five forces' model has economic origins in the structure-conduct-performance paradigm, resource-based theory has an economic base, but has found its inspiration in different places and further back in history. The framework draws on the Ricardian approach to the determination of economic rent, and the view of the firm as a collection of capabilities described by Edith Penrose and George Richardson.

Economic rent is what firms earn over and above the cost of the capital employed in their business. The terminology is unfortunate. It is used because the central framework was set out by David Ricardo in the early part of the 19th century, when agriculture was the dominant form of economic activity. Economic rent has been variously called economic profit, super-normal profit and excess profit – terms which lack appeal for modern business people. Most recently Stern Stewart, a consultancy, has had some success marketing the concept of economic rent under the label economic value added. The problem here is that value added – the value added that is taxed – means something different. Nor does my own attempt (in *Foundations of Corporate Success*) to call it added value help. Perhaps economic rent is best. The title doesn't matter. The concept does.

The objective of a firm is to increase its economic rent, rather than its profit as such. A firm which increases its profits but not its economic rent – as through investments or acquisitions which yield less than the cost of capital – destroys value.

In a contestable market – one in which entry by new firms is relatively early and exit by failing firms is relatively quick – firms which are only just successful enough to survive will earn the industry cost of capital on the replacement cost of their assets. Economic rent is the measure of the competitive advantage which effective established firms enjoy, and competitive advantage is the only means by which companies in contestable markets can earn economic rents.

The opportunity for companies to sustain these competitive

advantages is determined by their capabilities. The capabilities of a company are of many kinds. For the purposes of strategy the key distinction is between distinctive capabilities and reproducible capabilities. Distinctive capabilities are those characteristics of a firm which cannot be replicated by competitors, or can only be replicated with great difficulty, even after these competitors realise the benefits which they yield for the originating company.

Government licences, statutory monopolies, or effective patents and copyrights, are particularly stark examples of distinctive capabilities. But equally powerful idiosyncratic characteristics have been built by companies in competitive markets. These include strong brands, patterns of supplier or customer relationships, and skills, knowledge and routines which are embedded in teams.

Reproducible capabilities can be bought or created by any firm with reasonable management skills, diligence and financial resources. Most technical capabilities are of this kind. Marketing capabilities are sometimes distinctive, sometimes reproducible. The importance of the distinction between distinctive and reproducible capabilities for strategy is that only distinctive capabilities can be the basis of sustainable competitive advantage. Collections of reproducible capabilities can and will be established by others and therefore cannot generate rents in a competitive or contestable market.

* * *

So the strategist must first look inward and identify the distinctive capabilities of the organisation and seek to surround these with a collection of reproducible capabilities, or complementary assets, which enable the firm to sell its distinctive capabilities in the market in which it operates.

While this is easier said than done, the method defines a structure in which the processes of strategy formulation and its implementation are bound together. The resource-based view of strategy – which emphasises rent creation through distinctive capabilities – has found its most widely accepted popularisation in the core competencies approach of C. K. Prahalad and Gary Hamel. But that application has been made problematic by the absence of sharp criteria for distinguishing core and other competencies, which reopens the door to the wishful thinking characteristic of vision and mission-based strategising. Core competencies become pretty much what the senior management of the corporation wants them to be.

The perspective of economic rent – which forces the question 'why can't competitors do that?' into every discussion – cuts through much of this haziness. Characteristics such as size, strategic vision, market share and market positioning – all commonly seen as sources of competitive advantage, but all ultimately reproducible by firms with competitive advantages of their own – can be seen clearly as the result, rather than the origin, of competitive advantage.

Strategic analysis then turns outward, to identify those markets in which the company's capabilities can yield competitive advantage. The emphasis here is again on distinctive capabilities, since only these can be a source of economic rent, but distinctive capabilities need to be supported by an appropriate set of complementary reproducible capabilities.

Markets have product geographic dimensions, and different capabilities each have their own implications for the boundaries of the appropriate market. Reputations and brands are typically effective in relation to a specific customer group, and may be valuable in selling other related products to that group. Innovation based competitive advantages will typically have a narrower product focus but may transcend national boundaries in ways that reputations cannot. Distinctive capabilities may dictate market position as well as market choice. Those based on supplier relationships are frequently most appropriately deployed at the top of the market, while the effectiveness of brands is defined by the customer group which identifies with the brand.

Since distinctive capabilities are at the heart of competitive advantage, every firm asks how it can create distinctive capabilities. Yet the question contains an inherent contradiction. If irreproducible characteristics could be created, they would cease to be irreproducible. What is truly irreproducible has three primary sources: market structure which limits entry; firm history which by its very nature requires extended time to replicate; tacitness in relationships – routines and behaviour of 'uncertain imitability' – which cannot be replicated because no-one, not even the participants themselves, fully comprehends their nature.

So companies do well to begin by looking at the distinctive capabilities they have rather than at those they would like to have. And established, successful companies will not usually enjoy that position if they do not enjoy some distinctive capability. Again, it is easy to overestimate the effect of conscious design in the development of firms and market structures. The illusion of control strikes again.

* * *

This view of strategy, with its emphasis on the fit between characteristics and environment, links naturally to an evolutionary perspective on organisation. Organisms, or companies, which have capabilities matched to their requirement, emerge from processes which provide favourable feedback for characteristics which are well adapted to their environment. Both biological evolution and the competitive market economy are such processes.

Recent understanding of evolutionary systems emphasises how little intentionality is required to produce these results. Successful companies are not necessarily there because (except with hindsight) anyone had superior insight in organisational design or strategic fit. Rather, there were many different views of the firm capabilities a particular activity required: and it was the market, rather than the visionary executive, which chose the match that was most effective. Distinctive capabilities were established, rather than designed.

This view is supported by detached business history. Andrew Pettigrew's description of ICI shows an organisation whose path was largely fixed – both for good and for bad – by its own past. The scope and opportunity for effective management strategic choice – both for good and for bad – was necessarily limited by the past. This is not to be pessimistic about the potential for strategic direction or the ability of executives to make important differences, but to reiterate the absurdity and irrelevance of attempting to write corporate strategy on a blank sheet of paper. The resource-based view of strategy has a coherence and integrative role that places it well ahead of other mechanisms of strategic decision making.

A selection of the principal recent contributions to the view of business strategy described here is to be found in the items marked by an asterix in the bibliography.

Companies of the future

5 JANUARY 2000

Perhaps it was an alcoholic haze, perhaps a version of the Millennium Bug. But over the year-end celebrations I thought I saw a copy of the *Financial Times* for 31 December 2099. It may provide some clues to business trends in the next century.

There was a profile of the world's largest employer – the Educational Corporation of America. ECA was founded in 2005 when a group of parents and teachers in Seattle organised a buy out of a group of local schools. In the bad old days, the article explained with incredulity, the normal means of instruction had been for individual teachers, largely ignorant of educational research or technique, to harangue groups of thirty or forty inattentive students.

ECA's success was based largely on its management skills. It had also pioneered new educational technologies, constantly updated and developed in its international research centres. By the end of the twenty-first century one young person in three in the United States, and many more elsewhere, had enrolled in the ECA programme. Following a franchise agreement with the State of California in 2022, the ECA Berkeley had rapidly become the world's leading institution of higher education. ECA universities in both advanced and poor economies were generally leaders in their fields: the era of branded education had arrived.

Memphis-based General Genetics was the world's largest life sciences company. Following the genetic revolution in the early decades of the century, in which knowledge of gene and cell development had transformed medicine and nutrition, many companies had entered the new business of managed life care.

Traditional pharmaceutical companies and agribusinesses had mostly fallen by the wayside. After a decade or so, the industry had consolidated around a few companies – some previously established in other industries, some new – and General Genetics had emerged as market leader.

Once personal space travel became economic in the mid twenty-first century, many companies, mostly supported by national governments, had entered the business of space capsule construction and operation. The huge losses of these corporations dwarfed even the sums which had been lost in the conventional aviation business in the hundred years before.

But one profitable corporation stood out from the rest – Planetary Networks. It did not manufacture capsules, or provide sources directly to users. The company had developed space management systems which enabled individuals to plan safe, uncongested journeys. Although many more sophisticated techniques of space management had been proposed – the Intergovernmental Space Agency Union had spent decades discussing the ideal intergalactic system for the twenty-third century – the rapid adoption by users of PN software had given the company an unassailable lead over its competitors. Planetary Networks was a truly international company. It had no corporate headquarters in a traditional sense, and was registered under the liberal, and secretive, regime of the South American Economic Union.

Bengal Customware was one of PN's principal suppliers. In the first two decades of the century, leadership of the software industry had moved from the western United States to the Indian sub-continent: as the market matured, the competitive advantage of a cheap but well-educated labour force became overwhelming.

* * *

In business history, firms and industries change, but many principles remain the same. New industries emerged in the twentieth century from new technologies – automobiles, aircraft, electronics – and from the application of commercial organisation to activities previously undertaken in different ways – as in law and accountancy, consultancy, and waste disposal. We can expect both these developments to continue in the twenty-first century. Hence General Genetics and the Educational Corporation of America.

In the 1980s and 1990s privatisation and deregulation have created new industries and utilities. Once private businesses, then state controlled, are private businesses once more. The telecommunications sector was the darling of the stock market in 2000: in 1980 there was one telecommunication stock – AT&T. Medicine, education and transport infrastructure are the next opportunities.

Activities at the frontiers of today's fundamental research are plausible candidates for tomorrow's commercial development. That makes biology – the most exciting area of modern science – such a plausible basis for new industries next century. Yet we should not assume that advances in knowledge or capabilities can be translated into business success easily, or at all. The twentieth century has seen disappointing progress in fuel technologies. Nuclear fission reached commercial development, only to prove an economic and political failure: fusion, fuel cells and new devices for storing electricity have never reached major commercial application at all. As a result, Shell and Exxon end the twentieth century still enjoying the dominant position in their businesses that they held at the beginning of it.

Yet getting these social and scientific predictions right is not a sure route to business success. It is currently fashionable to think that large profits can be made by identifying new industries and investing in them. It is undeniably true that some people – from John D. Rockefeller to Bill Gates – have made a lot of money by controlling firms which became dominant in newly established sectors. But new industries, as a whole, are not more profitable than others: only more risky. They attract numbers of entrants that match their growth prospects and most of the entrants fall by the wayside.

Leaders ultimately emerge from this process as the shape of a new industry becomes evident, and the nature of competitive advantage in it is defined. The pioneers rarely become the leaders. Ultimately, the leader defines the standard – sometimes, not often, controlling the standard as Westinghouse did, Microsoft does and Planetary Networks might. More often, firms like General Motors and IBM define, for the period of their hegemony, the business model for their industry.

New industries have usually emerged first in already advanced economies and, as they reach maturity, their activities are transferred, first through sub-contracting and then completely, to poorer economies. This process will continue, with the result that China, India and other countries will play a far larger role in the future corporate economy than they do today. Hence Bengal Customware.

★ ★ ★

At this point, the haze lifted and the Bug departed. You will have to work out the rest of the century for yourself.

Bibliography

Andrews, K.R. (1965), *The Concept of Corporate Strategy*, Irwin Homewood, IL.

Angell, M. (2004), *The Truth about the Drug Companies: how they deceive us and what to do about it*, New York, Random House.

Ansoff, H.I. (1965), *Corporate Strategy*, New York, McGraw Hill.

*Barney, J. (1991), 'Firm Resources and Sustained Competitive Advantage', *Journal of Management,* 17.

Branson, R. (2000), *Losing my Virginity: the autobiography*, London, Virgin Books.

Burns, T. & G. M. Stalker (1961), *The Management of Innovation*, London, Tavistock Publications.

Chandler Jr, A.D. (1962), *Strategy & Structure: chapters in the history of the industrial enterprise*, Cambridge, MA, MIT Press.

Collins, J. (2001), *Good to Great*, London, Random House.

Desmet, D. *et al.* (2000), 'Valuing dot.coms', *McKinsey Quarterly*, No. 1.

Dunlap, A.J. with B.C. Andelman (1996), *Mean Business: how I save bad companies and make good companies great*, New York, Fireside.

Ford, H. & S. Crowther (1922), *My Life and Work,* Garden City, NY, Garden City Publishing.

Gates, B. with N. Myhrvold & P. Rinearson, (1995), *The Road Ahead,* London, Viking.

Glassman, J.K. & K.A. Hassett (1999), *Dow 36,000: The new strategy for profiting from the coming rise in the stock market*, London, Random House.

Goozner, M. (2004), *The $800 Million Pill: the truth behind the cost of new drugs,* Berkeley, CA, University of California Press.

Hamel, G. & C.K. Prahalad (1994), *Competing for the Future,* Cambridge, MA, Harvard Business School Press.

Handy, C.E. (1976), *Understanding Organisations*, London, Penguin.

*Hoopes, D. G., T.L. Madsen, G. Walker (eds) (2003), 'Why is there a resource-based view? Toward a theory of competitive heterogeneity', *Strategic Management Journal*, 24, pp. 889-902.

Iacocca, L. (1996), *Iacocca: an autobiography*, Bantam Books.

Kanter, R.M. (1989), *When Giants Learn to Dance*, New York, Touchstone.

*Kay, J.A. (1993), *Foundations of Corporate Success*, Oxford, Oxford University Press.

*Kay, J.A. (1996), *The Business of Economics*, Oxford, Oxford University Press.

Khurana, R. (2002), *Searching for a Corporate Saviour*, Princeton, NJ, Princeton University Press.

Le Carré, J. (2001), *The Constant Gardener*, London, Hodder and Stoughton.

Levitt, T. (1986), *The Marketing Imagination*, New York, The Free Press.

*Lippmann, S.A. & R. P. Rumelt (1982), 'Uncertain imitability: an analysis of interfirm differences in efficiency under competition', *Bell Journal of Economics, 23*.

Mair, A. (1999), 'Learning from Honda', *Journal of Management Studies*, vol.36, Issue 1.

Milgrom, P. & J. Roberts (1992), *Economics, Organisation and Management*, London, Prentice-Hall International.

Mintzberg, H. (1979), *The Structuring of Organisations,* Englewood Cliffs, Prentice-Hall.

Mintzberg, H. & J.A. Waters (1985), 'Of strategies, deliberate and emergent', *Strategic Management Journal* 6 (3), pp. 257-272.

Mintzberg, H. (2004), *Managers not MBAs*, FT Prentice-Hall.

*Montgomery, C.A. (1995), 'Of diamonds and rust' in C.A. Montgomery (ed.), *Resource-based and evolutionary theories of the Firm*, Boston, Kluwer.

Monteverde, K. & D. J. Teece, (1982), 'Supplier switching costs and vertical integration in the US auto industry', *Bell Journal of Economics*, 13/1, pp. 206-13.

Nathan, J. (1999), *Sony – the Private Life*, New York, HarperCollins.

Penrose, E.T. (1995, 3rd edn), *The Theory of the Growth of the Firm*, Oxford, Oxford University Press.

*Peteraf, M.A. (1993), 'The cornerstones of competitive advantage: a resource-based view', *Strategic Management Journal*, 14, vol. 3 March pp 179-91.

Peters, T.J. & R.H. Waterman (1982), *In search of excellence: lessons from America's best-run companies*, New York, Harpers & Row.

Pettigrew, A. (1985), *The Awakening Giant*, Oxford, Blackwell.

Porter, M.E. (1980), *Competitive Strategy: techniques for analysing industries and competitors,* New York, The Free Press.

Porter, M.E. (1985), *Competitive Advantage: creating and sustaining superior performance*, New York, The Free Press.

Porter, M.E. (1990), *The Competitive Advantage of Nations,* London, Macmillan.

Prahalad, C.K. & G. Hamel (1990), 'The core competence of the corporation', Harvard Business Review, May–June pp. 79-91.

Ricardo, D. (1971), *On the Principles of Political Economy and Taxation, 1817,* ed. R. M. Hartwell, Harmondsworth, Penguin.

Richardson, G.B. (1972), 'The organisation of industry' , *Economic Journal*, vol. 82, September, pp. 883-896.

*Rumelt, R.P., D. Schendel & D.J. Teece (1991) 'Strategic management and economics', *Strategic Management Journal*, 12 (Winter), pp 75-94.

Scherer, F.M. & D. Ross (3rd ed. 1990), *Industrial Market Structure and Economic Performance*, Boston, MA, Houghton Mifflin.

*Scherer, F.M. (1970), *Industrial Market Structure and Economic Performance*, Boston, MA, Houghton Mifflin.

Sloan, A. (1990, 1ˢᵗ ed. 1963), *My Years with General Motors,* New York, Doubleday.

Sperling, R. (1992), *Legend and Legacy: the story of Boeing and its people,* New York, St Martin's Press.

Sun Tzu (1993 ed.) *The Art of War*, Ware, Wordsworth Editions.

Tirole, J. (1988), *The Theory of Industrial Organisation,* Boston, MA, MIT Press.

Welch, J. (2001), *Jack: What I've Learned Leading a Great Company and Great People*, Headline.

*Wernerfelt, B. (1984), 'A resource-based view of the firm', *Strategic Management Journal,* 5.

Index

Everlasting Light Bulbs

184 pp. THE ERASMUS PRESS, 2004
ISBN 0-954-80930-0

Can economics be fun? Is it relevant to everyday life? John Kay believes passionately that the answer to both questions is yes and in this collection of essays, based on his widely acclaimed *Financial Times* columns, he sets out to prove it. In this book, you will learn why modern advertisements frequently convey no information, understand that tailgating drivers and hedge fund managers are victims of the same illusions, appreciate the inefficiency of Christmas giving, and benefit from the economic lessons of a romantic evening at the Elizabeth restaurant thirty years ago. You will find here acerbic commentary on the boom and bust in financial markets, a wide-ranging guide to the latest economic ideas, and a demonstration that complex analysis can be made accessible through lucid exposition and dry humour.

The economics of everyday life
The global economy
Risks and decisions
Economic systems
Economic policy
In defence of economics

Foundations of Corporate Success

416 pp. OXFORD UNIVERSITY PRESS, 1993
ISBN 0-19-828988-X

What distinguishes the successful firm is the fundamental question in British strategy, and one the most senior managers consistently ask themselves. In *Foundations of Corporate Success*, John Kay argues that outstanding businesses derive their strength from a distinctive structure of relationships with employees, customers, and suppliers. He explains why continuity and stability in these relationships is essential for a flexible and co-operative response to change. This book has been hailed as a landmark in our understanding of business strategy and is widely used on courses throughout the world.

Corporate success
Business relationships
Distinctive capabilities
From distinctive capabilities to competitive advantage
Competitive strategies
The strategic audit
The future of strategy

The Truth About Markets

496 pp. ALLEN LANE THE PENGUIN PRESS, 2003
ISBN 0-140-29672-7
(published in the United States as *Culture and Prosperity*
by HarperBusiness)

In the 1980s America won the cold war. In 1989 the Berlin Wall fell. The decade that followed proved one of the most extraordinary periods in economic history. The American business model – the unrestrained pursuit of self-interest, market fundamentalism, the minimal state and low taxation – offered its followers the same certainties that Marxism had given its own adherents for the previous century. There was a New Economy.

It was all to end in a frenzy of speculation, followed by recrimination and self-doubt. Corporations that had never earned a cent of profit, and never would, were sold to investors for billions of dollars. Corporate executives would fill their pockets and invent revenues and profits to support their accounts of their own genius. And every international economic meeting would be besieged by demonstrators.

In this ambitious and wide-ranging book, John Kay unravels the truth about markets, exploring the link between culture and prosperity. He shows that market economies function because they are embedded in a social, political and cultural context, and cannot work otherwise. These links explain why market economies outperformed socialist or centrally directed ones, but also why the imposition of market institutions often fails. But this is no dry academic treatise: Kay's quest takes him from the shores of Lake Zürich to the streets of Mumbai, through evolutionary psychology and moral philosophy, to the flower market at San Remo and Christies' saleroom in New York.

The Truth about Markets examines the big questions of economics – why some countries and people are rich, and others poor, why businesses succeed and fail, the scope of markets, and their limits. Witty yet profound, immersed in the most recent economic thinking yet completely accessible, it is both a tract for our times and a text for a new political economy.

REVIEWS

'A comprehensive, well-structured and highly readable exploration of markets and how they work.' *The Scotsman*

'This is quite possibly the only book on economics you will ever need to read.' **Stefan Stern,** *Accounting and Business*

'It offers one of the most truthful and fruitful ways in years of looking at the relationship between modern government and the modern economy.' **Martin Kettle,** *The Guardian*

'A landmark work.' **Will Hutton,** *Management Today*

'Written with wit and subtlety.' **Martin Vander Weyer,** *The Daily Telegraph*

'An ambitious and brilliantly executed book.' **Richard Lambert,** *The Times*

'A welcome antidote to the one-dimensional, reductionist accounts of the business world.' **Simon Caulkin,** *The Observer*

'John Kay's book explains some of the major economic topics of our time – indeed of all time.' **Joseph Stiglitz, Nobel Prize Laureate in Economics, 2001**

'John Kay provides a remarkable explanation of difficult ideas in simple and clear language – everything you wanted to know about economics but were afraid to ask.' **Mervyn King, Governor of the Bank of England.**

www.johnkay.com

This website is a comprehensive guide to John Kay's activities and writing. On it you can

- read and download a wide range of John Kay's articles

- search for materials on selected subjects

- receive advance notice of new publications

- order existing publications

- learn about current and coming events involving the author

- discover what is currently on John Kay's bookshelves

- obtain biographical and career details